THE
QUICK AFTER-WORK
WINTER
VEGETARIAN
COOKBOOK

THE
QUICK AFTER-WORK
WINTER
VEGETARIAN
COOKBOOK

JUDY RIDGWAY

PIATKUS

First published in 1996 by
Judy Piatkus (Publishers) Ltd
5 Windmill Street, London W1P 1HF

Paperback edition published 1997

The moral right of the author has been asserted

*A catalogue record for this book is available from
the British Library*

ISBN 0–7499–1658–3 (pbk)
ISBN 0–7499–1772–5 (hbk)

Designed by Paul Saunders
Illustrations by Madeleine David

Jacket photograph by Steve Baxter shows
oriental vegetable casserole with okra (page 74)
and carrot soup (page 52) with croutons

Typeset by Wyvern Typesetting Ltd, Bristol
Printed and bound in Great Britain by
Bookcraft Ltd, Midsomer Norton, Somerset

Contents

INTRODUCTION page 1

1 APPETIZERS & CANAPES page 9

2 FIRST-COURSE SOUPS page 23

3 HOT & COLD STARTERS page 36

4 MAIN COURSE SOUPS page 47

5 PIES & BAKES page 60

6 CASSEROLES & CURRIES page 71

7 FILLING FOOD page 85

8 SUPPER DISHES page 97

9 VEGETABLE ACCOMPANIMENTS page 110

10 WINTER SALADS page 123

11 SNACKS page 135

INDEX page 149

Introduction

I HAVE really enjoyed writing this book on *winter* vegetarian cooking because it has made me stop grabbing the nearest attractive-looking vegetable on the supermarket shelf and made me start to think about which vegetables really are in season at this time of year.

Of course, nowadays you can buy almost anything at any time of year but it is often at some cost to the pocket and perhaps at even greater cost to the environment. I have not renounced all out-of-season produce in this book but I have tried to make a feature of our own winter vegetables, spiced with a selection of other northern-hemisphere produce. This has certainly not restricted me very much. The range of fruit, vegetables and salads grown in the winter months has increased tremendously over the last few years.

Because of the plethora of choice it is not always easy to know, at any one time, exactly what is in season. I have therefore included a seasonal guide on pages 3–4. This is probably not completely comprehensive as market gardeners, in particular, are trying out new produce all the time. In October, while I was writing this book, I visited a market garden in Berkshire and the gardeners were planting a range of Japanese salad greens for sale later in the year.

At first sight, it might seem sensible to buy ready-made food from the supermarket chiller or freezer shelves when you are in a hurry. But recent research has shown that many meat-free convenience foods – like vegetarian burgers and sausages – have more fat, and are more expensive, than their meat counterparts. Other dishes have lost some of their vitamin and mineral content through long processing.

The best solution is to cook your own food. But vegetarian cooks are as busy as anyone else so quick cooking was an essential requirement for all the recipes in this book. I am very pleased that I have managed to come up with well over 100 recipes which really are quick to prepare and cook. Each dish takes just half an hour or less.

When I started on this project I thought it would be quite a challenge because so many winter vegetables take a long time to cook. But do they? Once I started developing recipes for the book, I began to see that long slow cooking was not the only way to deal with them.

We all know that winter greens have traditionally been over-cooked and that they really do benefit from fast methods of cooking, but what about root vegetables? Carrots, parsnips, swede and celeriac do take longer to cook if they are left whole but if you cut them into small pieces, or grate them, then they will cook very much more quickly. I have used this simple fact in many of the recipes that follow.

For example, root vegetables stir-fry very well if they are cut into matchsticks or, better still, into thin but wide shavings. For the latter, you will need to buy a tool which looks rather like a wide potato peeler on a small frame. You use it just like a continental cheese slicer.

For soups, stews and casseroles it is sufficient to dice root vegetables. If the dice are small they will cook in 15–20 minutes on top of the stove. If you are using root vegetables in fillings and stuffings you will need to cook them very quickly. This means coarsely grating, then cooking them in boiling water over a medium heat.

Some of the goodness of the vegetables leaches out into the water with this last method of cooking but it does give you some very well-flavoured vegetable water to add to stock or to use as it is in soups and stews.

This is particularly useful because it is difficult to find good vegetarian stock cubes. There are quite a few brands on the market but they taste rather artificial if they are not diluted with plenty of vegetable water, and some recipes need a strong stock.

I try to save all the cooking liquor from vegetables, however they are cooked. This is then used on its own, or to make a more strongly flavoured stock with yeast extract or other vegetables. I have given a recipe for a well-flavoured general stock on page 6. It can be used for any of the recipes in the book.

Freeze the prepared stock in ice cube trays and small plastic containers rather than large ones. You will then be able to select the amount you want to add to a dish without having to thaw a large quantity first.

Thinking ahead in this way really does help in speedy cooking. Equally, a well-planned storecupboard can help to turn a fairly ordinary meal, based on a few vegetables, some tofu or cheese and a filler like rice or pasta, into a really interesting culinary experience.

There is a list of some of the storecupboard and flavouring ingredients used in this book on page 5. Many of the items included, such as chopped chilli peppers in oil, Mexican spice paste, coconut cream, canned beans, chickpeas and tomatoes, and frozen chopped herbs, take a lot of the work out of food preparation. Keep your eyes open in supermarkets and delicatessens, as more useful ideas are appearing all the time.

If you are a strict vegetarian you will want to use cheeses which do not contain animal-based rennet. A list is given on pages 5–6. This may not be a comprehensive list, as more and more cheeses are being produced in this way. If you buy from a specialist cheesemonger he or she should know how a particular cheese was made.

Some of the recipes in this book include lightly cooked eggs. If you are worried about the risk of salmonella poisoning you may wish to avoid these dishes, especially if you are cooking for young children, elderly people or pregnant women.

If you are a vegan, look for the symbol Ⓥ next to the recipe titles. This denotes recipes which either do not use, or give alternatives to, ingredients of animal origin.

NOTES
Unless otherwise stated:
◆ All the recipes are for 4 people.

◆ The eggs are size 1.

◆ The spoon measures are flat rather than heaped.

Seasonal Vegetables/Fruits

VEGETABLES:

Beetroot	All year round
Broccoli	All year round
Brussels Sprouts	September to March
Cabbage and Spring Greens	One kind or another available throughout the year

Carrots	September to March
Cauliflower	All year round
Celeriac	September to April
Celery	September to March (best after winter frosts)
Chicory, Belgian	September to February
Fennel	July to March
Garlic	After October (mainly dried)
Jerusalem Artichokes	October to April
Kale	November to May
Kohlrabi	October to March
Leeks	August to May
Marrows	August to November
Mushrooms, farmed	All year round
Mushrooms, fresh wild	September to December, thereafter dried
Onions	All year round
Parsnips	August to April
Potatoes, main crop	September to June
Pumpkins	August to December
Spinach	All year round
Swede	September to May
Watercress	All year round but affected by extreme cold

FRUIT AND NUTS:

Apples	New season September onwards
Chestnuts	October to January
Pears	New season September onwards

Storecupboard Ingredients and Flavourings

I have assumed that your storecupboard already contains common items such as canned tomatoes and tomato purée, canned beans and chickpeas, pasta, rice, olive oil, soy and Tabasco sauces and the usual range of herbs and spices. Most of the following items are available in larger supermarkets but you may need to go to specialist shops for one or two of them.

INGREDIENTS:
Bulgur or cracked wheat and couscous
Canned coconut milk or coconut cream
Canned roasted chestnut purée
Capers
Cranberry jelly
Curried fruit chutney
Dried wild mushrooms
Polenta or cornmeal (quick-cook or ready-made)
Peanut, walnut or almond butter
Sesame seeds
Sherry vinegar
Sun-dried tomatoes (in oil or dried)
Taco shells
Tahini paste
Tamarind and date chutney
Tapenade or black olive paste (check to see that it does not contain anchovies)
Tortillas (corn or dried)
Vacuum-packed cooked whole chestnuts

FLAVOURINGS:

Black mustard seeds
Chopped chilli peppers in oil
Chopped lemon grass in oil
Fenugreek seeds
Five spice powder or paste
Frozen chopped herbs
Grated horseradish
Mexican spice paste
Oriental roasted sesame oil
Saffron strands
Star anise
Tamarind paste

Vegetarian Cheeses

Beenleigh Blue ewe's milk cheese
Berkswell ewe's milk cheese
Bonchester, 75g (3oz) size only
Capricorn
Devon Garland
Ducketts Caerphilly
Gubbeen
Harbourne Blue goat's milk cheese
Innes Clifton Ash goat's milk cheese
Lanark Blue
Lincolnshire Poacher
Llangloffan
Loch Arthur

Perroche goat's milk cheese
Pinn soft cheese
Ragstone goat's milk cheese
Smarts Single Gloucester
Smoked Wedmore
Spenwood ewe's milk
    cheese
Tornegus
Waterloo
Wealdon soft cheese
Wedmore
Wellington
Wigmore ewe's milk cheese
Yarg

Well-Flavoured Soup Stock

THIS IS the only recipe in the book which takes longer than half an
hour to prepare and cook. I usually get it going while I am preparing the evening meal and leave it to simmer while we eat. It can then be
strained and the implements washed up with the supper dishes.

You can, of course, make this useful stock with plain water, but I save
all the cooking liquor from boiling or steaming vegetables and use it to
add to the flavour.

If you do not have very much in the kitchen from which to make the
stock you can pep it up a little by adding some yeast extract. You will
need to take care, however, as most yeast extracts have very distinctive
flavours of their own and you do not want this taste pervading all your
cooking!

——— INGREDIENTS ———

1 tablespoon cooking oil
1 large onion, coarsely chopped (but not
    peeled)
2 large carrots, scrubbed (but not
    peeled) and coarsely chopped
4 sticks celery, trimmed and coarsely
    chopped

a small bunch of parsley, with the stalks
1 bayleaf
a pinch of dried thyme
salt and freshly ground black pepper
1 litre (1¾ pints) water or vegetable
    water

1. Heat the oil in a large saucepan until it is very hot. Add the onion, together with its skin, and fry for 1–2 minutes, allowing the onion to brown well.

2. Reduce the heat and add the carrots and celery. Continue to fry gently over a low heat for about 5 minutes. The mixture should not brown any further.

3. Add the herbs and seasoning. Stir and add the water or vegetable water. Bring the mixture to the boil and reduce the heat. Cover and simmer for 1–1½ hours. Strain, cool and store.

VARIATIONS

◆ You can use up any vegetables which are past their best in the stock. But take care with swede and the cabbage and cauliflower families, as they can add a very particular taste. This is fine if the stock is to be used with these vegetables but may not go so well with other ingredients.

◆ Add a little tomato purée to the stock for dishes which use tomatoes.

— CHAPTER ONE —

Appetizers & Canapés

QUITE a few of the recipes in this chapter were developed when I was running a small catering company. We often catered for small parties and our clients wanted interesting vegetarian nibbles to accompany their drinks.

When researching ideas for these menus, I found that very few books had any vegetarian party ideas other than cheese straws, cheese on sticks and cheese dips. There were certainly no vegan recipes. So I decided to adapt recipes from a variety of different cuisines to fit the party theme. Thus there are dips from India, Mexico and Russia; Spiced Banana Biscuits from the Caribbean and canapés from the United States, Greece and France.

Some of the recipes, such as Bhurta Dip and Fennel and Olive Tapenade, are quite versatile and can be used to make small canapés or larger finger food or even be pressed into service as first course dishes.

The secret of successful party nibbles is attractive presentation. Serve the food in small batches and arrange it on interesting leaves such as lamb's lettuce or radicchio. Alfalfa sprouts or mustard and cress also offer a pretty background.

Bhurta Dip

❖

THIS thick aubergine mixture from the Indian sub-continent makes an excellent hot dip to serve as an appetizer, a filling for little tartlets or as a topping for hot canapés.

When I can find them at specialist food shops I serve toasted Swedish Polarthins or Eskimo Rounds with this dip – they are a real talking point at a party. If these are not available you can always use chapatis or pitta bread.

INGREDIENTS

1 medium-sized onion, peeled and
  finely chopped
2 large cloves garlic, peeled and crushed
¼ teaspoon whole cumin seeds
¼ teaspoon ground cinnamon
seeds from 2 cardamom pods
2 cloves

2 tablespoons cooking oil
2 aubergines, peeled and very finely
  diced
2 large tomatoes, skinned and chopped
400ml (14fl oz) yogurt or silken tofu
salt and freshly ground black pepper
175g (6oz) frozen peas

---

1. Fry the onion, garlic and spices in the cooking oil for 4–5 minutes. Add all the remaining ingredients except the peas, and bring to the boil, stirring all the time.

2. Cover and cook over a medium heat for 20 minutes, stirring from time to time. Meanwhile cook the peas as directed on the pack. Drain and keep on one side.

3. Remove the mixture from the heat and mash with a potato masher. Stir in the peas, correct the seasoning if necessary, and serve.

Olive and Mascarpone Dip

SERVE this rich and flavoursome dip with potato crisps, nachos or, best of all, slices of toasted Italian ciabatta bread. It makes a good appetizer with pre-dinner drinks, an excellent late-night snack or an unusual party dip.

If you cannot find Mascarpone cheese, you can substitute any kind of cream cheese but the end result will not be quite so creamy.

INGREDIENTS

12 stuffed green olives
12 large black Kalamata olives
250g (9oz) Mascarpone cheese

4 tablespoons milk
1 teaspoon paprika pepper
salt and freshly ground black pepper

1. Stone and chop all the olives very finely and stir into the cheese.

2. Add all the remaining ingredients and mix well together. Serve in a bowl, with crisps, nachos or slices of toast arranged around it.

VARIATIONS
♦ Use 2 tablespoons drained and washed capers in place of the black olives and add some freshly chopped basil.

♦ Use 12 cocktail gherkins in place of the stuffed green olives and add some freshly chopped dill.

Mexican Mint and Chickpea Purée

I USE A food processor to make a rustic purée which is quite coarse. If you prefer a smoother finish, purée the chickpeas with the lemon juice in a blender.

Serve this with plain nachos – they show off the deliciously fresh taste of the purée much better than those which are finished with spices and other rather artificial flavourings.

Spoon the purée into a large bowl and place this in the centre of a large round or oval plate. Surround with nachos and decorate with radish and spring onion flowers which can also be dipped into the purée.

INGREDIENTS

1 × 400g (14oz) can chickpeas, drained
juice of 1 large lemon
a large bunch of mint, including at least
  12–15 sprigs

4–5 tablespoons extra virgin olive oil
salt and freshly ground black pepper

1. Rub the chickpeas through a sieve or purée them in a food processor or blender. Stir in the lemon juice.

2. Strip the leaves from the mint, retaining 1 sprig for decoration, and chop finely. Stir into the purée, with the olive oil and seasoning.

3. Add more lemon juice or oil to taste. If it is too thick but the flavour is good, add a little water to thin the mixture.

4. Spoon into a serving bowl and garnish with the reserved sprig of mint. Serve with the nachos.

Russian Bean Purée on Mini Oatcakes

❖

HERE is a tasty topping for mini oatcakes inspired by a Russian dish. It is very quick and easy to make. It can be used at once or you can store it in the fridge for a day or so. Be warned: if you do keep it, the flavour of the raw onions can get quite strong.

INGREDIENTS

1 × 225g (8oz) can red kidney beans, drained
25g (1oz) walnuts, chopped
½ bunch spring onions, trimmed and chopped

leaves from 4–5 large sprigs of fresh mint
salt and freshly ground black pepper
3 tablespoons lemon juice
20 mini oatcakes

◆

1. Place the kidney beans in a food processor with the walnuts and spring onions and chop roughly. Do not make the mixture too smooth. If you do not have a food processor you can rub the beans through a sieve, chop the walnuts, mince the spring onions and mix together.

2. Chop half the mint and stir into the mixture with the seasoning and the lemon juice.

3. Pile a spoonful of mixture onto each mini oatcake and garnish with small pieces of fresh mint.

VARIATIONS

◆ Use fresh dill in place of mint and add a few finely chopped cocktail gherkins.

◆ Use pinenuts in place of walnuts and parsley in place of mint.

Fennel and Olive Tapenade ⓥ

❖

THE best olives to use for this recipe are large Kalamata olives from Greece. You can either buy plain olives and add your own flavourings or buy herb-flavoured olives and simply add the cooked fennel to them.

This mixture is very versatile. It can be served on canapés with decorative slices of Feta cheese and a basil leaf or on toasted ciabatta bread under slices of grilled peppers, tomatoes or aubergine. In this case, you will not need to cool the mixture in the fridge.

——— INGREDIENTS ———

a 300g (10oz) head fennel
100g (3½oz) large black Kalamata olives
½ teaspoon dried thyme
4–6 whole coriander seeds, crushed

a pinch of ground dried bayleaf
freshly ground black pepper
2 tablespoons olive oil

1. Trim the fennel, removing any coarse outer layers, and chop well. Place in a pan and cover with boiling water. Bring to the boil again and cook for 7–8 minutes until tender.

2. While the fennel is cooking, stone the olives. Drain the fennel well, keeping the cooking liquor for stock. Dry the fennel on kitchen paper and purée in a blender with the stoned olives.

3. Stir in all the remaining ingredients and pop in the fridge to cool. Use as required after about 15 minutes.

Mushroom Bites

TAKE a tip from the States and serve your first course with the drinks in the form of tasty appetizers. These Mushroom Bites also make very good finger food.

Look for small mushrooms which are just opening at the gills. These are easier to stuff than closed cup mushrooms. They look particularly attractive served on a bed of green leaves such as baby spinach or lamb's lettuce.

INGREDIENTS

250g (9oz) full-fat cream cheese
2 teaspoons freshly grated root ginger
1 teaspoon freshly grated orange rind
4 tablespoons freshly chopped chives or spring onions

salt and freshly ground black pepper
500g (1lb 2oz) small mushrooms (around 30)
8–10 stuffed green olives, thickly sliced
a few whole chives

1. Mash the cream cheese with a fork and beat in the ginger and orange zest, chives or spring onions and seasoning.

2. Remove the stalks from the mushrooms and chop very finely. Stir into the cheese mixture.

3. Place a teaspoonful of the cheese mixture in each mushroom. Decorate with slices of stuffed olive. Insert a cocktail stick in each mushroom.

4. Arrange the stuffed mushrooms on a serving plate and decorate with a few whole chives.

Tomatoes Stuffed with Feta Cheese

IF YOU use small to medium-sized tomatoes for this, they make good bite-sized finger food.

―――――――――――― INGREDIENTS ――――――――――――

6–8 small to medium-sized tomatoes
115g (4oz) Feta cheese
115g (4oz) cottage cheese
2 tablespoons freshly chopped parsley

1 teaspoon dried thyme
salt and freshly ground black pepper
6–8 stuffed green olives, cut in half

1. Cut the tomatoes in half and scoop out the centres and seeds. Discard any hard pieces and chop the rest.

2. Mix the Feta and cottage cheese with the herbs and seasoning and moisten with the retained tomato.

3. Spoon the mixture into the tomato halves and decorate each one with half an olive.

VARIATIONS

♦ Chop the olives into the mixture and decorate with sprigs of flat-leaf parsley instead.

♦ Use finely chopped spring onions in place of parsley and freshly chopped mint instead of the dried thyme.

Avocado and Sweetcorn Canapés Ⓥ

❖

THIS crunchy and appetizing mixture can be served on rounds of toasted bread or on Mexican nachos. It can also be piled into ready-made pastry or vol-au-vent cases. It is fairly spicy, but it is quite easy to pep up or tone down the flavour by increasing or decreasing the amounts of fresh chilli and coriander.

This quantity makes enough to serve four as a first course or eight to ten as canapés. It is easy to double up the quantities for larger parties.

INGREDIENTS

1 x 200g (7oz) can sweetcorn or Mexicorn, drained
2 small tomatoes, skinned and chopped
4 spring onions, trimmed and finely chopped
½ small fresh red chilli, seeded and finely chopped
3 tablespoons freshly chopped flat-leaf parsley

1 tablespoon freshly chopped coriander
2 heaped tablespoons sour cream or puréed tofu
salt and freshly ground black pepper
1 ripe avocado, peeled, stoned and diced
a few sprigs of flat-leaf parsley

◆

1. Mix all the ingredients, except the avocado and the sprigs of parsley, in a large bowl. Keep in the fridge until required.

2. Just before serving prepare the avocado and add it to the mixture.

3. Pile onto your chosen base and decorate with the sprigs of flat-leaf parsley.

Egg and Tarragon Canapés

THIS mixture makes a very good topping for lightly seared slices of ciabatta or French bread. I sometimes use a hob grill brushed with a little oil to give the toast a rather attractive striation.

The mixture also makes an excellent dip for crudités – add a little more mayonnaise if using it in this way. Or it can be stuffed into split mini pitta breads with a few lettuce leaves.

INGREDIENTS

4 eggs

4 large sticks celery, very finely chopped

6–8 spring onions, very finely chopped

4 large sprigs of fresh tarragon, chopped

3 tablespoons capers, washed and coarsely chopped

115ml (4fl oz) mayonnaise

salt and freshly ground black pepper

a few small black olives

1. Boil the eggs for about 10 minutes until they are hard-boiled. Peel and plunge into cold water to cool. The eggs will be ready to use after 10–15 minutes.

2. Prepare your toast, crudités or pitta breads.

3. Chop the eggs (or mash them if using as a dip) and place in a bowl. Add the celery, spring onions, tarragon, capers and mayonnaise and season to taste with a little salt and plenty of black pepper. Mix well.

4. Pile the mixture onto the prepared base and garnish with small black olives.

Spiced Banana Biscuits Ⓥ

❖

THESE unusual cocktail bites are particularly quick to make. They are very versatile because they can be served on their own, with hummus or with a simple sour cream dip.

Spiced Banana Biscuits are best eaten while they are still warm, but they are pretty good cold too! Left-over biscuits make an excellent crumble topping for Coconut Bean Stew (see page 73).

INGREDIENTS

1 banana, peeled and mashed with a
  fork
300g (10oz) self-raising flour
1 teaspoon mild curry powder

¼ teaspoon baking powder
salt
40g (1½oz) butter or margarine, melted
cooking oil

◆

1. Place the mashed banana in a bowl and add all the remaining ingredients except the cooking oil. Add 4–5 tablespoons water. Using your fingers, mix to form a smooth pastry-like dough, adding a little more water if the texture is too crumbly.

2. Shape the dough into sausages about 2.5cm (1 inch) in diameter and slice into thin biscuits.

3. Pour 0.5cm (¼ inch) cooking oil into a frying pan and fry 10 biscuits for about ½ minute on each side until well browned. Remove from the pan and dry on kitchen paper.

4. Add more oil to the pan and continue to fry the biscuits in batches until all the dough has been used. Serve at once.

Cheese Dreams

CHEESE Dreams was the name I gave fried cheese and chutney sand-wiches when I was running a catering business in London. This very simple and easy-to-prepare finger food became the most popular item on my drinks party menu.

Here are three of my favourite combination fillings for the sandwiches but there are many other possibilities. Just use your favourite chutney or add a few herbs or spices and the taste will be quite different. For example, if you do not have a curried fruit chutney you can simply add a little curry paste or powder to your regular chutney.

—————————— INGREDIENTS ——————————

450g (1lb) grated Cheddar cheese
4 tablespoons Branston pickle

12 slices of white bread
115g (4oz) butter, softened

1. Mix the Cheddar cheese and pickle, or your chosen filling ingredients, together in a bowl.

2. Butter the slices of bread.

3. Place 6 slices of bread butter-side down on a sheet of baking paper. Spread with the filling mixture and top with the remaining slices of bread, butter-side up.

4. Cut each sandwich into 4 quarters and each quarter into 2 triangles.

5. Fry the sandwich triangles in a frying pan over a medium heat until well browned on each side.

VARIATIONS

♦ Use 4 tablespoons curried fruit chutney instead of the pickle and add 2 tablespoons freshly chopped mint.

♦ Use smoked Cheddar cheese in place of the ordinary Cheddar and 2 tablespoons cranberry jelly in place of half the pickle.

Glamorgan Sausages

THESE delicious little cheese sausages are rather like a Welsh version of Belgian Fondue, but instead of having to make a thick sauce you use breadcrumbs to hold the cheese. Of course, this makes for much faster preparation.

Small sausages disappear very fast at parties. Larger sausages served on a bed of mixed salad leaves make an excellent first course to serve before Mushroom Goulash with Noodles (see page 72).

INGREDIENTS

225g (½lb) grated Caerphilly cheese
175g (6oz) fresh breadcrumbs
6 spring onions, trimmed and finely
  chopped
4 tablespoons freshly chopped parsley
½ teaspoon dried thyme

salt and freshly ground black pepper
2 teaspoons made English mustard
4 small eggs (size 4), beaten
dry breadcrumbs
2 tablespoons cooking oil

1. Mix the cheese, fresh breadcrumbs, spring onions, herbs, seasoning and mustard with about half the beaten egg to make a thick paste which can be shaped.

2. Shape the mixture into 12 small or 6–8 larger sausages. Dip each sausage in the remaining egg and then coat with the dry breadcrumbs.

3. Heat the oil in a pan and fry the sausages for 2–3 minutes until well browned all over. Drain on kitchen paper and serve at once.

VARIATION

♦ For an even more authentic Welsh flavour, use a small leek in place of the spring onions. Baby leeks are even better. You will need 3–4.

Japanese Tofu Canapés

Most wholefood shops now offer a choice of Japanese or Chinese-style tofu. I usually buy the Japanese style for this recipe, as it is more open-textured and takes up the marinade rather well. However any kind of plain tofu can be used.

The marinated tofu tastes delicious but it does need a pretty presentation to set it off. Try arranging the canapés on a bed of alfalfa and use as many toppings as possible to achieve a colourful effect.

——————————————— INGREDIENTS ———————————————

1 × 350g (12oz) block plain tofu
five spice powder
4 tablespoons light soy sauce
1 tablespoon roasted sesame oil
2 teaspoons cider vinegar or white wine
   vinegar
2 teaspoons freshly grated root ginger
freshly ground black pepper
2 tablespoons cooking oil
1 cucumber, thickly sliced

TOPPINGS

grated mooli mixed with paprika pepper
creamed horseradish
finely chopped red and green peppers
chopped Japanese pickled ginger
a few sprigs of fresh coriander

1. Cut the tofu into 8 slices and sprinkle each side of each slice with the five spice powder. Arrange on the base of a flat dish.

2. Mix the soy sauce, sesame oil, vinegar, ginger and pepper together and spoon over the tofu. Leave to stand for 15–20 minutes, turning the tofu slices from time to time.

3. Heat the oil in a large frying pan. Dry the tofu slices on kitchen paper and fry on each side for about 1 minute. The slices should be lightly browned.

4. Cut each slice into 4 pieces and place each piece on a slice of cucumber. Decorate with a mixture of your chosen toppings.

CHAPTER TWO

First-Course Soups

I LOVE soups, particularly in the winter. They get the meal off to a great start. My husband likes his soups chunky and I like them smooth and creamy so here is a choice of both types.

Among the clear soups there are Chinese Fragrant Soup and Thai Soup with Lemon Grass and Coriander; chunky vegetable soups include Quick Winter Borscht and Chickpea Broth with Coriander; and thick puréed soups take in Crème Dubarry with Leeks, and Chestnut and Orange Soup.

These soups have been devised and tested as first course soups, but some of them, such as Spanish Lenten Soup and Broad Bean and Hazelnut Soup, are often served as the main part of the meal in the areas from which they come. If you would like to do this simply double the quantities of all the ingredients except the vegetable stock. Add more stock as the mixture cooks if you think it is getting too thick.

Chinese Fragrant Soup Ⓥ

❖

THIS fragrant Chinese-style stock can be served on its own with a simple garnish of silken tofu cubes and chopped spring onions or it can be used as a base for other Oriental soups.

The longer you can boil the mixture the better, but it will have sufficient flavour to use after about 20 minutes. If you are able to cook the stock for a longer period, reduce the heat to a slow boil. Make a double or treble quantity and freeze for quick use another day.

——————————— INGREDIENTS ———————————

1 tablespoon cooking oil
1 onion, coarsely sliced, with the skin on
1 carrot, thinly sliced
5cm (2 inch) piece of fresh root ginger, peeled and thinly sliced
1 tablespoon soy sauce

1 bayleaf
a large bunch of parsley
a few sprigs of thyme
a piece of star anise or a pinch of five spice powder

1. Heat the oil in a wok or deep pan and fry the vegetables until lightly browned.

2. Add all the remaining ingredients, together with 1.2 litres (2 pints) water, and bring to the boil. Boil over a medium heat for 20 minutes.

3. Strain and use as required.

Thai Soup with Lemon Grass and Coriander Ⓥ

❖

THIS aromatic soup makes a wonderful first course for any Oriental meal. Thai ingredients such as lemon grass and fresh coriander are now widely available. Tamarind paste can be found in ethnic grocers and some specialist delicatessens. If you cannot find it, use lemon juice instead.

INGREDIENTS

1 teaspoon tamarind paste
1 fresh green chilli
1 dried red chilli
1 piece lemon grass
2 slices lime
1 vegetable stock cube
1 onion, peeled and coarsely sliced

2 carrots, peeled and sliced diagonally
1 tablespoon cooking oil
4 broccoli spears, chopped
50g (2oz) beansprouts
1 tablespoon soy sauce
a few fresh coriander leaves

◆

1. Pour 900 ml (1½ pints) water into a saucepan and add the tamarind, chillies, lemon grass, lime and stock cube. Bring to the boil and simmer for 20 minutes.

2. In another pan gently stir-fry the onion and carrots in the oil for 2 minutes. Add the broccoli and continue to stir-fry for a further minute.

3. Strain the soup and return to the saucepan. Add the stir-fried vegetables, beansprouts and soy sauce and bring to the boil. Serve garnished with the fresh coriander leaves.

Oriental Egg and Tomato Soup

THIS is really an East-meets-West dish from California and I am not at all sure about its Eastern origins! However it makes an interesting first course for an Oriental meal.

─────────────── INGREDIENTS ───────────────

900ml (1½ pints) Chinese Fragrant Soup (see page 24)

4 tomatoes, each cut into about 8 wedges

4 spring onions or a small bunch of chives, very finely chopped

1 tablespoon dark soy sauce

1 egg

a few drops of roasted sesame oil

1 tablespoon dry sherry

a few sprigs of flat-leaf parsley

1. Heat the Chinese Fragrant Soup in a deep saucepan and add the tomatoes. Simmer for 5 minutes.

2. Add the spring onions or chives and the soy sauce and bring back to the boil.

3. Beat the egg in a cup and pour in a steady stream into the boiling soup.

4. Just as the egg sets, spoon the soup into 4 bowls. Sprinkle with the sesame oil and dry sherry, garnish with the parsley and serve at once.

Chickpea Broth with Coriander

❖

THE unusual flavour of this Greek soup depends on the whole dried coriander seeds. Resist the temptation to add fresh coriander as a garnish. The fresh herb will take over completely.

Serve as a first course with plenty of sesame-seed-topped Greek bread.

INGREDIENTS

1 tablespoon whole coriander seeds, lightly crushed

2 tablespoons extra virgin olive oil

2 onions, peeled and sliced

1 × 400g (14oz) can chickpeas

115g (4oz) small button mushrooms, halved or quartered

1 teaspoon dried oregano

1 bayleaf

115ml (4fl oz) white wine

300ml (½ pint) tomato juice

400ml (14fl oz) vegetable stock

salt and freshly ground black pepper

---

1. Fry the coriander seeds in the olive oil for 30 seconds. Add the onions and continue to fry gently for another 2–3 minutes.

2. Add the contents of the can of chickpeas and all the remaining ingredients. Bring to the boil and cook, uncovered, for 15–20 minutes.

3. Check that the onions are cooked, and serve at once.

Quick Winter Borscht

❖

A MEDLEY of root vegetables is the basis for this Russian-inspired soup. It has a wonderful deep red colour and an interesting sweet and sour flavour. Non-vegans might like to add a dollop of sour cream just before serving.

INGREDIENTS

1 onion, peeled and finely sliced
1 large carrot, peeled and grated
1 small white turnip, peeled and grated
1 stick celery, trimmed and very finely sliced
2 tablespoons vegetable oil
900ml (1½ pints) vegetable stock

salt and freshly ground black pepper
225g (½lb) cooked beetroot, grated
2 teaspoons lemon juice
1 teaspoon tomato purée
½ teaspoon sugar
sour cream (optional)

1. Gently fry all the vegetables, except the beetroot, in hot vegetable oil for 2–3 minutes to soften a little.

2. Pour on the stock and seasoning and add the beetroot. Bring to the boil and simmer for 20–25 minutes.

3. Stir in the lemon juice, tomato purée and sugar. Ladle into bowls and serve at once. If liked, add a dollop of sour cream on top of each portion.

Spanish Lenten Soup

❖

THE Lenten fast, during which people avoid meat, is strictly observed in many parts of Spain. At this time chickpeas prepared in this way are extremely popular. I usually serve this soup as a first course, as I find that too many chickpeas are a bit too much of a good thing! But if you would like to follow the Spanish custom and serve the soup as a main course, you can simply increase the ratio of vegetables to liquid.

INGREDIENTS

1 clove garlic, peeled and crushed
1 small onion, peeled and chopped
2 tablespoons olive oil
a few strands of saffron
3 tomatoes, skinned, seeded and
 chopped

500ml (18fl oz) vegetable stock
1 × 400g (14oz) can chickpeas
450g (1lb) spinach, shredded
salt and freshly ground black pepper

◆

1. Fry the garlic and onion in the olive oil to soften. Add the saffron and fry for a further minute.

2. Next add the tomatoes and cook for a further 2–3 minutes to make a good paste.

3. Stir in the stock, then add the chickpeas, spinach and seasoning. Cover and cook over a low heat for about 10 minutes.

Broad Bean and Hazelnut Soup ⓥ

THIS is a good standby soup when you're in a hurry. Simply raid the freezer for the broad beans and the storecupboard for the nuts. If you do not have hazelnuts to hand, you can toast some flaked almonds, peanuts or even cashew nuts and grind these in the blender to use instead.

INGREDIENTS

1 onion, peeled and chopped
1 tablespoon cooking oil
50ml (2fl oz) sherry (optional)
500g (1lb 2oz) frozen broad beans

900ml (1½ pints) vegetable stock
salt and freshly ground black pepper
50g (2oz) ground hazelnuts
4 tablespoons yogurt or soya yogurt

1. Gently fry the onion in the oil in a saucepan until just golden. Do not allow the onion to burn. This will take 5–8 minutes.

2. If using sherry, add it to the onions now and bring to the boil. If not, add a teaspoon of sugar to sweeten the soup. Next add the broad beans, stock and seasoning. Bring the mixture to the boil. Reduce the heat, cover and simmer for the cooking time given on the pack of frozen beans.

3. Purée the soup in a blender or rub through a sieve.

4. Add the hazelnuts and return to the heat. Bring to the boil and serve at once with a swirl of yogurt or soya yogurt on each portion.

Crème Dubarry with Leeks

THIS variation on the traditional French Cauliflower Soup is particularly rich and creamy. Serve in small quantities with hot French bread and follow with Curried Lentils (see page 112) and Rice with Sweetcorn (see page 91).

INGREDIENTS

2 leeks, trimmed, cleaned and sliced
15g (½oz) butter
1 tablespoon cooking oil
1 glass sherry
1 cauliflower, broken into large pieces

1 teaspoon French mustard
salt and freshly ground black pepper
750ml (1¼ pints) vegetable stock
150ml (¼ pint) single cream
1 egg yolk

1. Fry the leeks in the butter and cooking oil for 2–3 minutes.

2. Pour in the sherry and bring to the boil. Add the cauliflower, mustard, seasoning and stock and bring back to the boil. Cover and simmer for 20 minutes. Sieve or blend the soup and return to the pan.

3. Mix the cream and egg yolk together and pour into the soup. Heat through, stirring all the time. Serve just before the mixture comes to the boil. If you allow the mixture to boil, the egg and cream mixture will curdle.

VARIATION

◆ Use 115g (4oz) blue cheese instead of the cream and egg yolk to give a piquant but still creamy taste. I have tried it with Beenleigh Blue, a vegetarian ewe's milk cheese, but you could use Harbourne Blue vegetarian goat's cheese, Stilton or Roquefort.

Portuguese Caldo Verde Ⓥ

❖

IN PORTUGAL this soup is always made with a very fibrous cabbage rather like kale, but you can use any kind of shredded green cabbage.

Serve with country bread and complete the meal with Celeriac and Ricotta Filo Pie (see page 63).

INGREDIENTS

1 onion, peeled and sliced
2 tablespoons olive oil
350g (12oz) potatoes, cubed
750ml (1¼ pints) vegetable stock

salt and freshly ground black pepper
225g (½lb) kale or green cabbage,
 shredded

---

1. Fry the onion in the olive oil for 2–3 minutes. Add the potatoes, vegetable stock and seasoning and bring to the boil.

2. Simmer for 15 minutes. Purée in a blender or rub through a sieve.

3. Add the shredded kale or cabbage and bring the soup back to the boil. Simmer for a further 10 minutes. Serve at once.

VARIATION

◆ Melt a small round Boursin cheese into the soup and serve as a main course, followed by a winter salad from Chapter 10.

Curried Celeriac Soup

❖

THIS simple soup makes a very effective first course when you are entertaining. Follow with Oriental Vegetable Casserole with Okra (see page 74), Sag Aloo with Greens (see page 82) and rice.

INGREDIENTS

1 large onion, peeled and sliced
1 tablespoon cooking oil
450g (1lb) celeriac, peeled and sliced
1 tablespoon curry powder

salt and freshly ground black pepper
900ml (1½ pints) vegetable stock
a few toasted pinenuts

1. Fry the onion in the cooking oil for 5–6 minutes until lightly browned. Add the celeriac and curry powder and continue frying for 2–3 minutes.

2. Add the seasoning and stock and bring to the boil. Simmer for 20 minutes until the celeriac is tender.

3. Toast the pinenuts, if you do not have them to hand, while the soup is cooking. Purée or sieve the soup, reheat, and serve garnished with the toasted pinenuts.

VARIATION
◆ Use half parsnip and half celeriac.

Leek and Mustard Soup with Mushrooms

❖

THIS recipe, which is now one of my favourites, came about quite by chance. I love leeks in any shape or form and while I was testing recipes for this book I decided to make a leek soup. On checking the vegetable compartment in the fridge for some balancing flavours I found some mushrooms which really needed using up. And the rest, as they say, is history.

INGREDIENTS

1 large onion, peeled and sliced

675g (1½lb) leeks, trimmed, cleaned and sliced

15g (½oz) butter or 1 tablespoon cooking oil

50ml (2fl oz) dry sherry (optional)

175g (6oz) button mushrooms, sliced

1 potato, peeled and chopped

1 tablespoon Dijon mustard

900ml (1½ pints) vegetable stock or water

salt and freshly ground black pepper

a little cream, yogurt or puréed silken tofu

◆

1. Gently fry the onion and the leeks in the butter or cooking oil for 2–3 minutes, stirring all the time.

2. Add the sherry, if using, and bring to the boil. Cook for 1 minute to remove the alcohol. Add two-thirds of the mushrooms, and the potato, mustard, stock or water, and seasoning. Bring the mixture to the boil. Cover, reduce the heat and simmer for 30 minutes.

3. Rub through a sieve or purée in a blender or food processor. Return to the heat, and add the remaining mushrooms. Bring to the boil and simmer for another 5 minutes.

4. Serve with a swirl of cream, yogurt or puréed silken tofu on each portion.

Chestnut and Orange Soup

❖

I USED a new brand of canned chestnut purée made with roasted chestnuts for this recipe. Both the colour and the flavour are much better than the purées made with unroasted chestnuts. Of course, you can also make this soup with the fresh chestnuts that are on sale during the autumn months but it will take much longer to prepare!

―――――――――――――― INGREDIENTS ――――――――――――――

1 small carrot, peeled and chopped
1 onion, peeled and chopped
100g (3½oz) mushrooms, chopped with
    their stalks
2 tablespoons cooking oil
1 × 400g (14oz) can chestnut purée

750ml (1¼ pints) vegetable stock
juice of 1 orange
salt and freshly ground black pepper
grated rind of 1 orange
some freshly chopped parsley

1. Fry the vegetables in the cooking oil for about 5 minutes until very lightly browned.

2. Add all the remaining ingredients, except the orange rind and parsley, and bring to the boil. Cover and cook over a medium heat for 15 minutes.

3. Purée in a blender or rub through a sieve, reheat, and serve garnished with the orange rind and parsley.

— CHAPTER THREE —

Hot & Cold Starters

Here is a selection of some of my favourite vegetarian first courses. Some, like the Chanterelles on Toasted Brioche, Warm Cauliflower and Caper Salad and Oriental Sweetcorn Fritters, are hot. Others, such as Cheese Pâté with Apples and Walnuts or Lemon Bean and Almond Salad, are cold.

There are also a number of other recipes scattered through the book which could be served as starters: Fennel and Olive Tapenade (see page 14) with tomatoes on bruschetta, Glamorgan Sausages (see page 21), Tofu and Tomato Platter Pies (see page 64), Spanish Stuffed Tomatoes (see page 66), Hard-Boiled Eggs in Onion Sauce (see page 100), Taco Salad (see page 129), Mushroom and Cheese Sauté (see page 140), to name but a few.

If you are really very short of time, grilled vegetables are always a good standby. Simply slice peppers, aubergines, courgettes, fennel, chicory and radicchio lengthways, brush with a little olive oil and pop under the grill. (They can be cooking and browning while you are making the main course.) When they are cooked, toss in extra virgin olive oil and freshly chopped herbs. They are very good served hot, tepid or cold.

Chanterelles on Toasted Brioche

THIS really is best made with fresh chanterelle mushrooms; dried ones simply don't have the same wonderful flavour. It is also important to use butter because it blends particularly well with the delicate flavour of the chanterelles. However, if you are determined to avoid butter, the dish is quite good cooked with extra virgin olive oil and a splash of tarragon vinegar in place of the butter and lemon juice.

This starter is extremely quick to make which makes it an ideal first course when you are entertaining. Follow it with Egg and Cabbage Parcels (see page 99) and Potato and Celery Stew (see page 78).

———— INGREDIENTS ————

4–6 shallots, peeled and finely chopped
2 cloves garlic, peeled and finely
    chopped
2 tablespoons olive oil
75g (3oz) butter
4 tablespoons freshly chopped parsley

2 sprigs of fresh tarragon, chopped
salt and freshly ground black pepper
115ml (4fl oz) white wine
225g (½lb) chanterelle mushrooms
4 thick slices of brioche
juice of ½ lemon

1. Fry the shallots and garlic in the oil and 25g (1oz) of the butter for 2 minutes. Add the herbs and seasoning and fry for another 2 minutes.

2. Next add the wine and boil off completely. This takes about 5–8 minutes.

3. Pick over the chanterelles, brush off any earth and wipe carefully. Toast the brioche.

4. Melt the remaining butter in another pan and toss the chanterelles in this for 1 minute. Add the shallot mixture. Toss and serve on the slices of toasted brioche.

5. Sprinkle with fresh lemon juice just before serving.

Crostini Porcini

❖

THIS recipe makes a very rich mixture which is particularly good when offset by a strongly flavoured salad vegetable such as rocket or water-cress. It can also be used to make canapés or finger food for a buffet.

Many supermarkets now stock Italian dried porcini mushrooms or you can buy them in specialist delicatessens. Other dried mushrooms can be used but the flavour will be a little different. Save the liquor in which the porcini have been reconstituted and use it to flavour soup or casserole stocks.

INGREDIENTS

7g (¼oz) dried porcini, soaked in boiling water for 15 minutes

2 tablespoons olive oil

1 small-to-medium onion, peeled and finely chopped

1 clove garlic, peeled and crushed

175g (6oz) button mushrooms, very finely chopped indeed

115g (4oz) open cup mushrooms, roughly chopped

50ml (2fl oz) vegetable stock

2 tablespoons dry white wine

1 large sprig of fresh marjoram, chopped

4 sprigs of fresh parsley, chopped

¼ teaspoon dried thyme

salt and freshly ground black pepper

1 tablespoon ground almonds

6 rounds of ciabatta bread

some rocket or watercress

◆

1. Finely chop the porcini and keep on one side.

2. Heat the oil and fry the onion and garlic until transparent. Add the finely chopped button mushrooms and fry again for 2–3 minutes.

3. Add the remaining mushrooms, including the porcini and a little of their soaking juices, the stock, the wine, herbs and seasoning and bring to the boil. Cook, uncovered, over a medium heat until nearly all the juices have evaporated.

4. Stir in the almonds and continue cooking for another minute. The mixture should be quite thick.

5. Meanwhile toast or fry the bread. When the porcini mixture has finished cooking pile it onto the crostini (crispy bread), garnish it with some rocket or watercress, and serve.

Oriental Sweetcorn Fritters

I USUALLY serve these highly spiced fritters on a bed of salad which has been dressed with a little oil and light soy sauce. The quantities given here will serve four people as a first course or two as a main course with stir-fried vegetables. If you want to make more, simply double up the quantities.

INGREDIENTS

250g (9oz) canned or cooked sweetcorn kernels
8–10 small spring onions, trimmed and chopped
2 cloves garlic, peeled and crushed
2.5cm (1 inch) piece of fresh root ginger, peeled and grated

a few drops of Tabasco sauce
3 tablespoons plain flour
½ teaspoon baking powder
salt and freshly ground black pepper
1 small egg, beaten
1 tablespoon cooking oil

1. Mix the sweetcorn kernels with the spring onions, garlic, ginger and Tabasco. Stir in the flour, baking powder, seasoning and beaten egg.

2. Heat the oil in a large frying pan and drop 8 spoonfuls of the mixture into the hot oil. Cook for 3–4 minutes on each side until the fritters are lightly browned. Serve at once.

Tofu Sesame Slices

THE longer you are able to marinate the tofu, the better it will taste. Serve on a bed of spicy leaves such as rocket or watercress. If you want to turn this into a supper dish add a good helping of Warm Spicy Noodle Salad (see page 88).

―――――――――――――― INGREDIENTS ――――――――――――――

1 × 350g (12oz) plain block tofu
2 tablespoons dark soy sauce
juice of ½ lemon
2 tablespoons freshly grated root ginger
1 clove garlic, peeled and cut in half

2 tablespoons plain flour
4 tablespoons sesame seeds
5 tablespoons olive oil
rocket or watercress

―――――――――――――――― ◆ ――――――――――――――――

1. Cut the block of tofu into 8 strips and place in a shallow dish.

2. Mix the soy sauce, lemon juice and ginger and pour over the tofu. Add the garlic to the marinade and leave to stand until required.

3. Mix the flour and sesame seeds and put on a plate. Dip the marinated tofu slices into the mixture and coat well on both sides.

4. Heat 2 tablespoons of the oil in a pan and fry the coated tofu slices on both sides. This will only take about a minute for each side. The coating should be lightly browned and crisp.

5. Arrange the salad leaves on individual plates and transfer the tofu slices to the plates with a fish slice.

6. Mix any remaining marinade with the rest of the olive oil and spoon over the top.

Grilled Pepper Ramekins with Hummus

❖

THE longer you can leave these ramekins in the fridge, the better they will keep their shape when you come to turn them out. However the flavour is just as good whatever shape they are in! Serve with toasted ciabatta or French bread.

─── INGREDIENTS ───

4 large red or mixed coloured peppers, seeded and cut into quarters
8 tablespoons hummus

4 large sprigs of fresh basil
salt and freshly ground black pepper
extra virgin olive oil

1. Place the pieces of pepper skin-side up under a hot grill and cook until well seared. It is not necessary to remove the skin but if you have time you may prefer to do so.

2. Line 4 small ramekin dishes with a third of the pieces of pepper. Place a tablespoonful of hummus in each, top with basil leaves, and season. Cover with more pepper pieces and then the remaining hummus, more basil and seasoning. Finish off with a final layer of pepper pieces.

3. Cover with cling film and place in the fridge until required. Turn out to serve on individual plates and decorate with the remaining basil leaves. Drizzle with some olive oil and serve at once.

Cheese Pâté with Apples and Walnuts

C HEESE pâté is extremely versatile. It can be served as an unusual first course in the way suggested below. It can also be spread on toasted croûtons or stuffed into ready-made pastry shells to serve as canapés or it can be used to make sandwiches.

—————— INGREDIENTS ——————

115g (4oz) fromage frais or quark
115g (4oz) Cotswold or other flavoured
   Cheddar cheese, grated
115g (4oz) savoury biscuits, crushed
freshly ground black pepper

2 green eating apples, peeled
juice of ½ lemon
6 walnut halves, chopped
sprigs of parsley or watercress

1. Mix both cheeses with the savoury biscuits and season with pepper. Press the mixture into a small basin or pâté dish. Cover and place in the fridge for 15 minutes or until required.

2. Core and slice the apples and place in a bowl with the lemon juice.

3. Remove the cheese pâté from the fridge and use 2 tablespoons to mould 8 oval shapes. Place 2 on each plate.

4. Arrange the apple slices at the side and sprinkle with the chopped walnuts. Garnish with a few sprigs of parsley or watercress.

Soft Lettuce Salad with Tapenade Croûtons and Artichokes

❖

IN THE dead of winter, soft greenhouse lettuce is the main salad ingredient and it certainly needs something to give it more interest. This recipe uses the piquant flavour of French tapenade to do just that.

Artichokes, too, have a very definite flavour of their own which blends well with the tapenade. I try to find artichoke bases rather than the often stringy artichoke hearts, but you could use artichokes in oil or a good artichoke paste spread on more ciabatta or French bread.

INGREDIENTS

2 thick slices of ciabatta or olive bread
extra virgin olive oil
3 tablespoons tapenade
soft lettuce leaves
6 canned artichoke bases, diced
4 sun-dried tomatoes, cut into strips

a few sprigs of fresh herbs, e.g. basil
and parsley

DRESSING
3 tablespoons extra virgin olive oil
1 teaspoon sherry vinegar
salt and freshly ground black pepper

---

1. Brush the bread with plenty of olive oil and toast under the grill or fry in a frying pan. Spread with the tapenade and cut into 20–24 small cubes.

2. Arrange the lettuce leaves on a serving plate and dot with the tapenade croûtons. Add the artichokes, sun-dried tomato strips and herbs.

3. Mix the dressing ingredients together and pour over the salad. Serve at once.

Watercress Salad with Mangetouts

❖

HOMEGROWN watercress is a great winter salad ingredient and mangetouts seem to be flown in all year round, so I decided to try putting the two together. Here's the very tasty result. Serve as a first course with wholemeal rolls.

─── INGREDIENTS ───

1 bunch or bag of watercress, picked
   over and washed
a few soft lettuce leaves, roughly torn
75g (3oz) mangetouts, trimmed, strung
   and cut into strips lengthways
4 sun-dried tomatoes, cut into strips
2 tablespoons pinenuts or flaked
   almonds, toasted

DRESSING
4 tablespoons extra virgin olive oil
2 teaspoons sherry vinegar
salt and freshly ground black pepper

1. Arrange the watercress and lettuce on 4 plates. Sprinkle with strips of mangetout and sun-dried tomato and the toasted nuts.

2. Mix the dressing ingredients with a fork, pour over the salad and serve at once.

Warm Cauliflower and Caper Salad Ⓥ

❖

THIS is a simple but very effective salad which makes a good first course for a special occasion. Follow with Fruity Cheese Parcels (see page 61) or Tofu and Tomato Platter Pies (see page 64).

INGREDIENTS

4 baby cauliflowers or ½ large one
1 thick slice of white or wholemeal bread
4 tablespoons herb- or garlic-flavoured olive oil
some mixed salad leaves
½ red or mild onion, peeled and thinly sliced into rings

2 tablespoons finely chopped fresh parsley
1 tablespoon capers, washed in cold water and drained
2 teaspoons cider vinegar or wine vinegar
salt and freshly ground black pepper

---

1. Set the oven to 200°C/400°F/Gas Mark 6.

2. Cut the baby cauliflowers in half or the larger one into 8 pieces. Steam over boiling water for 5–6 minutes to soften a little.

3. Place the bread on a baking tray and drizzle with about a tablespoonful of the flavoured olive oil. Bake for 5 minutes until crisp and golden. Cut into small squares.

4. Arrange the mixed salad leaves on 4 plates. Cut the steamed cauliflower into smaller chunks and place on the leaves. Scatter the croûtons, onion rings, parsley and capers over the top.

5. Beat the remaining olive oil with the vinegar and seasoning and spoon over each salad. Serve at once.

VARIATION

◆ Sprinkle the finished salad with a sieved hard-boiled egg.

Lemon Bean and Almond Salad

❖

THIS mixed bean salad makes a very colourful first course. It is based on a salad I first tried in a small restaurant in Provence. Surprisingly it contained no garlic which was something of a relief after the onslaught of that particular flavouring in the cuisine of Provence. Of course, if you love garlic there is no reason why you should not add a little!

—————————— INGREDIENTS ——————————

175g (6oz) flat green beans, trimmed and strung	25g (1oz) toasted flaked almonds
50g (2oz) French beans, trimmed	2 tablespoons olive oil
salt	juice of 1 lemon
75g (3oz) canned kidney beans, drained	a little grated lemon rind
	freshly ground black pepper

1. Cut both types of beans into 2.5cm (1 inch) lengths. Plunge into a pan of boiling salted water and cook for 5 minutes. Drain and cool under cold running water. Drain again and dry on kitchen paper.

2. Mix the cooked beans with the kidney beans and flaked almonds and spoon into a bowl.

3. Mix the olive oil, lemon juice, lemon rind and pepper with a fork and pour over the salad. Toss and serve.

VARIATION

♦ Use a small orange in place of the lemon and add a dash of cider vinegar or wine vinegar to the dressing.

CHAPTER FOUR

Main Course Soups

A STEAMING tureen full of thick nourishing soup is served as a main course in every country that features soup in its culinary repertoire. Add a few hunks of country bread and you have the makings of an excellent meal.

The main course soups in this chapter come from France, Italy, Germany, Poland, Britain and Mexico. They should all fill four hungry people. If you have a little extra time it is worth making a double quantity. You can then store the other half in the fridge or freezer to make another easy meal later in the week.

Recipes which lend themselves particularly well to this treatment are Soupe au Pistou (but make the Pistou freshly each time you serve the soup), Italian Bean Soup, Sweet and Sour Cabbage Soup, Italian Risotto Soup, Tomato Noodle Soup and Sweetcorn and Camembert Soup.

Soupe au Pistou

THE flavour of this wonderfully aromatic soup from Provence depends on using plenty of basil in the Pistou dressing. A 'bunch' in this part of the world means a lot more than a sprig or two. In fact, the more the better!

Vegans can make a very good soup by simply leaving out the Parmesan cheese and blending finely chopped tofu into the basil mixture instead.

Serve with plenty of crusty wholemeal bread and finish the meal with a compote of dried fruit.

INGREDIENTS

1 onion, peeled and chopped
1 large leek, trimmed, cleaned and sliced
1 tablespoon olive oil
1 large carrot, peeled and diced
3 tomatoes, skinned and chopped
2 small or 1 large courgette, sliced
75g (3oz) frozen sliced French beans
50g (2oz) macaroni or thick pasta shapes

salt and freshly ground black pepper
1 × 200g (7oz) can cannellini beans

PISTOU DRESSING
3 cloves garlic, peeled and chopped
a bunch of fresh basil
50g (2oz) freshly grated Parmesan cheese
2 tablespoons extra virgin olive oil

1. Gently fry the onion and leek in the oil until the onion softens. Add the carrot and toss in the oil. Cover with 600ml (1 pint) water and bring to the boil. Simmer for 10 minutes.

2. Add the tomatoes, courgette, French beans, pasta and seasoning and simmer for a further 10 minutes.

3. Add the cannellini beans and some more water if the soup is too thick. Cook for 5 more minutes.

4. Meanwhile, make the Pistou by grinding the garlic with the basil in a mortar and pestle or by processing in a blender. Blend in half the Parmesan cheese and oil and then stir in the rest.

5. Ladle the cooked soup into 4 bowls, top each one with a generous dollop of Pistou, and serve.

Italian Bean Soup

❖

THIS delicious soup from Tuscany is served on top of a good hunk of bread and the two together make a nutritious and filling main course. Finish off with a topping of your most robustly flavoured olive oil and complete the meal with a stuffed baked apple or apple tart.

INGREDIENTS

1 medium onion, peeled and finely chopped
1 clove garlic, peeled and finely chopped
1 tablespoon olive oil
4 tomatoes, skinned and chopped
2 sticks celery, thinly sliced
1 carrot, peeled and finely diced
3–4 large sprigs of parsley, coarsely chopped

½ teaspoon dried oregano or marjoram
½ small to medium-sized Savoy cabbage, about 450g (1lb) when trimmed
1 litre (1¾ pints) strong vegetable stock
salt and freshly ground black pepper
175g (6oz) canned cannellini or white haricot beans
4 large hunks of wholemeal bread
extra virgin olive oil

◆

---

1. Gently fry the onions and garlic in the olive oil until lightly browned. Add the tomatoes, celery, carrot and herbs and continue to fry gently for a further 4–5 minutes.

2. Now add the cabbage, stock and seasoning and bring to the boil. Cook over a medium heat for about 15 minutes until the cabbage is just tender. Stir in the beans and bring back to the boil.

3. Place the bread in 4 large deep soup bowls and ladle the soup on top. Serve with extra virgin olive oil to pour over.

Thick Cauliflower and Leek Soup

❖

THIS is another thick Italian vegetable soup served over hunks of bread. It comes from Pisa where the locals often add a sprinkling of Parmesan cheese, but this is not necessary if you want to avoid dairy produce.

Toast the bread until it is lightly seared for an even stronger flavour.

INGREDIENTS

2 onions, peeled and chopped
extra virgin olive oil
4 leeks, trimmed, cleaned and thickly
   sliced
1 small head of cauliflower, broken into
   large florets and the stems sliced
2 tomatoes, skinned and chopped

1 bayleaf
1 sprig of fresh rosemary or ¼ teaspoon
   dried rosemary
1 litre (1¾ pints) strong vegetable stock
salt and freshly ground black pepper
4 large hunks of coarse white country
   bread

1. Gently fry the onion in 2 tablespoons extra virgin olive oil until lightly browned. Add all the remaining vegetables and continue to fry gently for another 4–5 minutes.

2. Now add the herbs, stock and seasoning and bring to the boil. Cook over a medium heat for 15 minutes.

3. Place the hunks of bread in 4 large deep soup bowls and ladle the soup on top. Serve with extra virgin olive oil to pour over.

Italian Poached Egg Soup

KNOWN in Italy as *Zuppa alla Pavese*, this soup is said to have been served to one of the kings of Italy after he had been defeated in battle. It makes a warming main course and, for best results, you will need a good strong vegetable stock.

It is easiest to make it individually, but I have successfully served four by using a deep frying pan which is large enough to take four slices of bread.

INGREDIENTS

900ml (1½ pints) vegetable stock
4 slices of Italian white bread
2 tablespoons olive oil

4 eggs
4 tablespoons finely grated Grana
    Padano or Parmesan cheese

---

1. Heat the stock in a saucepan.

2. Brush both sides of the bread with the olive oil and pour the remaining oil into a large deep frying pan. Cook the bread on each side until well browned. Break an egg over each slice.

3. Slowly pour the boiling stock over the eggs and continue to baste them until the whites are set.

4. Carefully remove each slice of bread with its egg and place in a bowl. Pour on the soup, top with the grated cheese and serve at once.

Carrot Soup with Curd Cheese Dumplings

MAKING dumplings seems to be a dying art in Western Europe, though they are still very popular in Eastern Europe. These Polish dumplings are easy to make and very light and fluffy.

INGREDIENTS

1 onion, peeled and finely chopped
1 tablespoon cooking oil
500g (1lb 2oz) carrots, peeled and finely diced
2 sticks celery, diced
1 tablespoon tomato purée
750ml (1¼ pints) well-flavoured vegetable stock
1 bayleaf
salt and freshly ground black pepper

DUMPLINGS
1 egg, separated
15g (½oz) butter, softened
115g (4oz) curd cheese or sieved cottage cheese
2-3 spring onions, trimmed and finely chopped
2 tablespoons plain flour
¼ teaspoon ground cardamom seeds
salt and freshly ground black pepper

1. Start by making the soup. Gently fry the onion in the cooking oil to soften. Add the carrots, diced as finely as possible, and the celery and continue to fry gently for 3–4 minutes.

2. Add the tomato purée, stock, bayleaf and seasoning and bring to the boil. Cook over a medium heat for 15 minutes.

3. Meanwhile, make the dumplings. Put a large pan of water on to boil. Cream the egg yolk and softened butter with the cheese. Add the spring onions, flour and ground cardamom and season well.

4. Whisk the egg white until stiff and stir a tablespoonful into the cheese mixture. Then fold in the rest of the egg white.

5. Place 4 large tablespoonfuls of dumpling mixture on top of the boiling water and simmer very gently for 10 minutes, turning over once in that time. Transfer the dumplings to the soup with a slotted spoon and serve at once.

Broccoli Chowder

❖

A LARGE helping of this vegetable-packed chowder makes a good main course with wholemeal bread. Add crispy fried onion slices as an unusual garnish. You can make these yourself or buy them in supermarkets where they are often sold as salad garnishes.

INGREDIENTS

2 onions, peeled and sliced
15g (½oz) butter or 1 tablespoon
  cooking oil
1 head of broccoli or calabrese, broken
  into florets and the stems chopped
350g (12oz) new potatoes, scrubbed and
  quartered or diced
75g (3oz) frozen peas

75g (3oz) fresh or frozen sweetcorn
900ml (1½ pints) milk or soya milk
1 bayleaf
a pinch of dried mixed herbs
salt and freshly ground black pepper
2 tablespoons finely chopped fresh
  parsley

◆

1. Gently fry the onions in the butter or oil until they turn transparent and then add all the remaining ingredients, retaining a little parsley for decoration.

2. Bring the mixture to the boil and cover. Turn the heat down very low and simmer gently for 15–20 minutes until all the vegetables are tender. Ladle into 4 bowls, sprinkle with the remaining parsley, and serve.

VARIATIONS

◆ Use 75g (3oz) green beans in place of the peas.

◆ Use 75g (3oz) finely diced carrots in place of the sweetcorn.

Sweet and Sour Cabbage Soup

❖

THE inspiration for this hearty soup came from a visit to Bavaria where it is served with buttered black pumpernickel bread. Start the meal with Cheese Pâté with Apples and Walnuts (see page 42) or Grilled Pepper Ramekins with Hummus (see page 41).

INGREDIENTS

1 small green cabbage with the stalk removed, approximately 350g (12oz)
2 onions, peeled and sliced
1 very large potato, peeled and finely diced
1 large cooking apple, peeled and diced
600ml (1 pint) vegetable stock

300ml (½ pint) tomato juice
3–4 whole allspice or ¼ teaspoon ground allspice
salt and freshly ground black pepper
1 tablespoon dark muscovado sugar
juice of 1 lemon

---

1. Shred the cabbage very finely indeed and place in a saucepan with all the remaining ingredients except the lemon juice.

2. Bring the mixture to the boil, cover and simmer for 20 minutes until all the vegetables are tender.

3. Stir in the lemon juice, correct the seasoning if necessary, and serve.

VARIATION
♦ Use caraway seeds or juniper berries in place of allspice.

Italian Risotto Soup

Peas, tomatoes and rice are typical of the dishes of the Veneto and this recipe appears in an old family cookbook from that area. The main flavouring is dried fennel seeds which are quite difficult to find in the UK but some specialist and healthfood shops do stock them. If you cannot find them use fennel herb instead, or you could completely change the flavour and use dried oregano or celery seeds.

The longer you leave the soup to stand, the thicker it will become. Serve with plenty of freshly grated Parmesan cheese and black pepper. Yes, my Italian friends really do add black pepper to this particular dish!

INGREDIENTS

1 onion, peeled and very finely chopped
2 tablespoons extra virgin olive oil
4 large (but not beefsteak) ripe
    tomatoes, skinned and chopped
100g (3½oz) risotto or long-grain rice

600ml (1 pint) vegetable stock
salt and freshly ground black pepper
200g (7oz) frozen peas
freshly grated Parmesan cheese

1. Fry the onion in the extra virgin olive oil until it is soft. Add the tomatoes and continue cooking for another minute or so.

2. Stir in the rice and make sure it is well coated with the tomato mixture. Add the stock and seasoning, stir and bring to the boil. Cover and cook for 5 minutes.

3. Add the peas. Bring the mixture back to the boil and simmer for a further 10 minutes. Leave to stand for 5 minutes to allow the rice to take up more of the juices.

4. Serve with Parmesan cheese and black pepper on the side.

Tomato Noodle Soup Ⓥ

THIS is an unusual noodle soup in that it is not clear. Instead it is thickened with flour to give it a velvety texture.

I tested this recipe using thin Italian noodles (or spaghettini) but you could use Chinese thread noodles instead. Simply follow the cooking instructions on the packet. Remember that, whichever kind of noodles you use, they will continue to take up the liquid if they are left to stand after the end of the cooking time. If this happens simply add more stock.

─────────── INGREDIENTS ───────────

1 onion, peeled and chopped
1 small red pepper, seeded and chopped
1 tablespoon cooking oil
1 tablespoon plain flour
4 tomatoes, skinned and chopped
900ml (1½ pints) vegetable stock

100g (3½oz) noodles
1 tablespoon horseradish relish or
 1 teaspoon grated horseradish
salt and freshly ground black pepper
1 teaspoon cider vinegar

1. Gently fry the onion and pepper in the oil for 3–4 minutes without browning.

2. Stir in the flour and add the tomatoes. Stir again and then gradually add the stock. Bring the mixture to the boil and add all the remaining ingredients except the vinegar.

3. Bring to the boil again, cover and cook over a medium heat for about 15 minutes until the noodles are cooked.

4. Just before serving stir in the vinegar.

Mexican Potato Soup

❖

THIS homely but well-flavoured soup is really welcome on a cold winter's evening. Start the meal with Tofu Sesame Slices (see page 40) or Avocado and Sweetcorn Canapés (see page 17).

INGREDIENTS

2 onions, peeled and thickly sliced
2 cloves garlic, peeled and chopped
1 small fresh green chilli, seeded and
　finely chopped
2 tablespoons olive oil
1 × 225g (8oz) can tomatoes
750ml (1¼ pints) vegetable stock

450g (1lb) large potatoes, peeled and
　cubed
½ teaspoon dried oregano
salt and freshly ground black pepper
2 tablespoons freshly chopped coriander
juice of ½ lemon

---

1. Gently fry the onions, garlic and chilli in the olive oil until soft but not brown. Add the tomatoes and cook over a medium heat for 4–5 minutes.

2. Stir in the stock and then add the potatoes, oregano and seasoning. Bring to the boil and simmer for 20 minutes until the potato is tender.

3. Serve sprinkled with freshly chopped coriander and lemon juice.

VARIATION

◆ Add 1 small avocado, peeled, stoned and chopped, towards the end of the cooking time

Fennel Soup with Goat's Cheese

DESPITE the very definite taste of the two main ingredients, this nourishing soup is surprisingly delicate in flavour. If you have the time it is very good served with a sprinkling of fried breadcrumbs.

Look for heads of fennel which still have some greenery on them. You can reserve this and use it to garnish the soup.

INGREDIENTS

1 tablespoon olive oil
15g (½oz) butter
2 onions, peeled and sliced
450g (1lb) fennel, trimmed and cut into
    chunks
1 carrot, peeled and chopped
750ml (1¼ pints) vegetable stock
salt and freshly ground black pepper

175g (6oz) chèvre goat's cheese, rind
    removed

OPTIONAL GARNISH
6 tablespoons fresh breadcrumbs
2 tablespoons olive oil
a few sprigs of fennel herb

---

1. Heat the oil and butter in a pan and gently fry the onions for 2–3 minutes. Do not allow them to brown. Add the fennel and carrot and toss with the onions for a minute. Add the stock and seasoning and bring to the boil. Cover and simmer for 20 minutes.

2. If you are making the garnish, fry the breadcrumbs in the olive oil until well browned and keep on one side.

3. Rub the cooked soup through a sieve or purée in a blender. Grate the goat's cheese or cut it into small pieces and stir, a little at a time, into the hot purée. Reheat gently and serve garnished with fried breadcrumbs, if using, and sprigs of fennel herb.

Sweetcorn and Camembert Soup

YOU can use any kind of mild matured soft cheese in this very quick-to-make thick soup. Start the meal with Soft Lettuce Salad with Tapenade Croûtons and Artichokes (see page 43), serve the soup with crusty French bread, and finish with baked stuffed apples.

INGREDIENTS

2 × 200g (7oz) cans creamed sweetcorn
450ml (¾ pint) milk
115g (4oz) Camembert or similar cheese,
   rind removed

a good pinch of nutmeg
salt and freshly ground black pepper
freshly chopped parsley

1. Empty the cans of creamed sweetcorn into a saucepan and gradually stir in the milk.

2. Cut the cheese into small pieces and add to the soup with the nutmeg and seasoning. Stir over a medium heat until all the cheese has melted and the soup has heated through thoroughly.

3. Spoon into bowls and serve with a sprinkling of chopped parsley.

CHAPTER FIVE

Pies & Bakes

Filo pastry is the only kind of pastry which will cook properly in the time you have left after preparing the filling! It also has the advantage of being ready rolled out.

Some people are a little frightened of filo pastry but it is very easy to use. The secret is not to be shy of the butter or oil used to moisten each sheet. To get the best results, the pastry must be well brushed with fat before being cooked. However a little melted fat goes a long way.

As well as filo pies, I have included a number of stuffed vegetable dishes in this chapter. With the exception of tomatoes, the vegetables need a quick flash under the grill or in boiling water to soften them before they go into the oven.

Eggs cook very quickly in the oven and there are plenty of variations on the recipe for Egg and Vegetable Nests. The simplest method is to cook eggs *en cocotte* in flavoured cream, or cream and melted Boursin. Make sure that the liquid is almost at boiling point before you put it in the *cocotte* dishes. Break the eggs on top and cook at once.

Fruity Cheese Parcels

YOU can use any kind of soft rinded cheese for these crispy filo pastry parcels but a small log-shaped goat's cheese is the most convenient. (I used Ste-Mauré.) Add your favourite fruit chutney – the spicier the better.

Serve with stir-fried mangetouts to make an elegant main course. Start the meal with Spanish Lenten Soup (see page 29) or Broad Bean and Hazelnut Soup (see page 30) and finish with sliced oranges.

--------------------------- INGREDIENTS ---------------------------

2 × Ste-Mauré or other small log-shaped
   goat's cheese
12 sheets filo pastry

3–4 tablespoons olive oil
12 teaspoons plain or curried fruit
   chutney

1. Set the oven to 200°C/400°F/Gas Mark 6 and cut each cheese into 6 thick slices.

2. Brush each sheet of filo pastry with a little olive oil and fold in half. Brush and fold again, into a small 4-layered square.

3. Place a slice of cheese in the centre of each square and top with a spoonful of chutney.

4. Gather the corners of the pastry together over the cheese and pinch together with a little water. Place on a baking tray.

5. Continue making parcels until you have completed all 12. Place the baking tray in the oven and bake for 10–15 minutes until crisp and golden.

VARIATION

◆ If you do not have any chutney to hand, simply sprinkle the goat's cheese with a mixture of ground nutmeg and dried thyme or with freshly chopped mint or parsley.

Spinach and Chestnut Filo Pie

❖

THIS rather unusual recipe is based on a Southern Italian pasta filling, but it works just as well in filo pastry. I used canned roast chestnut purée which has a particularly good flavour, but any kind of unsweetened chestnut purée will do. And I usually use cream cheese but, if you prefer a lower fat content or do not want to use dairy food at all, silken tofu also works very well.

INGREDIENTS
---

olive oil

450g (1lb) fresh leaf spinach

250g (9oz) cream, curd or ricotta cheese
  or silken tofu

½ × 435g (15oz) can roast chestnut purée

juice and grated rind of ½ lemon

1 teaspoon dried thyme or oregano

1 teaspoon coriander seeds, crushed

salt and freshly ground black pepper

6 sheets filo pastry

◆

1. Set the oven to 200°C/400°F/Gas Mark 6 and brush a 28 × 18cm (11 × 7 inch) Swiss roll tin with olive oil.

2. Steam the spinach with very little water until it begins to wilt. Drain well and keep on one side.

3. Mix the cheese or tofu with the chestnut purée, lemon juice and rind, herbs, coriander seeds and seasoning. It should form a smooth creamy paste.

4. Line the Swiss roll tin with 3 layers of filo pastry, brushing each layer with oil as you go. Spoon on the chestnut mixture and then spread the spinach all over the top. Cover with 3 more layers of oil-brushed filo.

5. Cut into 8 squares with a sharp knife. Place in the oven and bake for 15 minutes. If you are in a hurry you could use 2 layers of filo above and below, rather than 3. The pie should then be ready in about 12–13 minutes.

VARIATION

◆ For a subtle Oriental feel substitute 2–3 tablespoons soy sauce for the lemon juice and add a pinch of five spice powder.

Celeriac and Ricotta Filo Pie

CELERIAC has a very delicate flavour which falls somewhere between celery and parsnips. Indeed in America the vegetable is known as celery root. You need to buy a large celeriac to get a reasonable amount of flesh, as the root usually needs quite a lot of trimming.

This mixture can also be used to make individual platter pies such as those on page 64.

INGREDIENTS

4 tablespoons olive oil
500g (1lb 2oz) celeriac, trimmed, peeled and coarsely grated
4 tablespoons white wine or vegetable stock
225g (½lb) ricotta cheese

40g (1½oz) sun-dried tomatoes, chopped
4 tablespoons freshly chopped parsley
salt and freshly ground black pepper
6 sheets filo pastry

1. Set the oven to 200°C/400°F/Gas Mark 6 and brush a 28 × 18cm (11 × 7 inch) Swiss roll tin with a little olive oil.

2. Make the filling by cooking the celeriac in the white wine or stock for 5–6 minutes. Boil fast and keep stirring. When the celeriac starts to soften, remove from the heat.

3. Mix the ricotta and sun-dried tomatoes in a bowl and add the cooked celeriac, parsley and seasoning.

4. Line the Swiss roll tin with 3 layers of filo pastry, brushing each layer with oil as you go. Spoon on the celeriac mixture and spread flat with a knife. Top with 3 more layers of oil-brushed filo.

5. Cut into 8 squares with a sharp knife. Place in the oven and bake for 15 minutes. If you are in a hurry you could use 2 layers of filo above and below, rather than 3. The pie should then be ready in about 12–13 minutes.

Tofu and Tomato Platter Pies

❖

FILO pastry pies can look very attractive if they are cooked in individual entrée dishes. I have an ovenproof set which is ideal. Each dish has a base diameter of 10cm (4 inches) and sloping sides to give a rim diameter of 14cm (5½ inches).

The mixture can also, of course, be used in a Swiss roll tin (see pages 62 and 63) if you do not have any suitable individual dishes.

INGREDIENTS

1 clove garlic, peeled and chopped
2 onions, peeled and chopped
6 tablespoons olive oil
4 tomatoes, skinned, seeded and chopped

1 × 300g (10oz) block plain tofu
3 tablespoons coarsely torn basil leaves
2 tablespoons tomato purée
salt and freshly ground black pepper
6 sheets filo pastry

---

1. Set the oven to 200°C/400°F/Gas Mark 6 and grease 4 individual entrée dishes.

2. To make the filling, fry the garlic and onions in 2 tablespoons olive oil in a small frying pan until lightly browned. Stir in the tomatoes and cook for another 2 minutes.

3. Place the tofu in a large bowl and mash with a fork. Add the contents of the frying pan, the basil, tomato purée and seasoning. Mix well.

4. Cut each filo pastry sheet into quarters. Line each entrée dish with 3 small pieces of filo pastry, brushing each layer with the remaining oil as you go. Spoon on the tofu and tomato mixture and spread flat with a knife. Top with 3 more layers of oil-brushed filo.

5. Place in the oven and bake for 15 minutes. If you are in a hurry you could use 2 layers of filo above and below, rather than 3. The pies should then be ready in about 12–13 minutes.

Soufflé Mushrooms

IT IS important to choose open cup mushrooms rather than flat field mushrooms because the rim of the cup helps to stop the soufflé mixture from overflowing into the baking dish. You can use any hard cheese such as Cheddar, Emmental or Gouda – each one will give a slightly different flavour.

INGREDIENTS

4 large open cup mushrooms
olive oil
75g (3oz) grated cheese
25g (1oz) fresh breadcrumbs
25g (1oz) walnuts or pecan nuts, finely
   chopped

2 eggs, separated
1 tablespoon thick soy sauce
1 teaspoon made mustard
salt and freshly ground black pepper

1. Set the oven to 200°C/400°F/Gas Mark 6 and put the grill on.

2. Remove the stalks from the mushrooms. Brush the caps with olive oil and place under the grill gill-side down. Cook for 5 minutes. Turn over and cook on the other side for the same amount of time.

3. Meanwhile, prepare the soufflé topping. Mix the cheese, breadcrumbs and nuts in a bowl. Stir in the egg yolks and all the remaining ingredients, except the egg whites. This will make quite a stiff mixture.

4. Whisk the egg whites until they are very stiff. Mix 2 tablespoonfuls into the cheese mixture, then fold in the rest.

5. Place the grilled mushrooms on an ovenproof dish, gill-side up, and pile some cheese soufflé mixture on top of each one. Place in the oven and bake for 10–15 minutes. Serve at once.

Spanish Stuffed Tomatoes Ⓥ

❖

Serve these large stuffed tomatoes with Spicy Stuffed Peppers (see page 67) or with Spinach Bake with Goat's Cheese (see page 68). Alternatively, you could double up the ingredients and serve two stuffed tomatoes per person as a main dish with Gingered Neeps (see page 116).

Use the left-over chickpeas in soup or toss them in garlic, parsley and lemon juice and serve on a bed of rocket as a tangy starter.

―――――――――――― INGREDIENTS ――――――――――――

4 large beefsteak tomatoes
100g (3½oz) canned chickpeas, drained
75g (3oz) sharply flavoured grated
   cheese (e.g. Pecorino or Caerphilly)

3 tablespoons freshly chopped coriander
salt and freshly ground black pepper

◆

1. Set the oven to 200°C/400°F/Gas Mark 6.

2. Cut the tops off the tomatoes and scoop out the seeds with a knife. Keep the tops on one side and discard any tough centres. Scoop out and chop the rest of the flesh and put in a bowl with the seeds.

3. Rub the chickpeas through a sieve or purée them in a food processor and add to the tomato. Stir in the cheese, coriander and seasoning. Mix to a thick paste.

4. Spoon this paste into the prepared tomato shells and cover with the tops. Place on an ovenproof plate and bake for 15 minutes. Serve at once.

Spicy Stuffed Peppers

❖

YOU can make these well-filled peppers as hot and spicy as you like, depending on your choice of curry powder. Serve with Spanish Stuffed Tomatoes (see page 66) and fresh noodles.

INGREDIENTS

4 red or green peppers
1 small onion, peeled and finely chopped
1 tablespoon olive oil
2 carrots, peeled and grated
½ × 400g (14oz) can chickpeas, drained
1 cooking apple, peeled, cored and
   grated

1 tablespoon mango chutney
1 tablespoon curry powder
salt and freshly ground black pepper
   (optional)
4–5 tablespoons vegetable stock

◆

1. Set the oven to 200°C/400°F/Gas Mark 6.

2. Cut the stalks and seeds out of the centre of the peppers and plunge into a large pan of boiling water. Boil fast for 7–8 minutes to soften but not wilt. Place in an ovenproof dish.

3. Fry the onion in the oil until lightly browned and add the carrots. Cook for another 2–3 minutes.

4. Rub the chickpeas through a sieve or purée in a food processor. Place in a bowl and add the fried vegetables, cooking apple, chutney and curry powder. Season if you wish, mix well and spoon into the prepared peppers.

5. Bring the stock to the boil and pour into the dish with the peppers. Place in the oven and bake for 15–20 minutes.

Spinach Bake with Goat's Cheese

THE yogurt, raisins and cinnamon give this dish a sweet and spicy tang which is very characteristic of South American food. The idea for the recipe came from Colombia but it could have been Peru or even Chile. Serve with Italian Braised Pumpkin (see page 119).

INGREDIENTS

450g (1lb) frozen chopped spinach
50g (2oz) raisins
200ml (8fl oz) thick yogurt
¼ teaspoon cinnamon
salt and freshly ground black pepper
115g (4oz) sweetcorn

175g (6oz) mature hard goat's cheese, grated
100g (3½oz) fresh breadcrumbs
a few knobs of butter
some freshly chopped chives

1. Set the oven to 220°C/425°F/Gas Mark 7.

2. Mix the chopped spinach in a small saucepan with the raisins, yogurt, cinnamon and seasoning. Place over a medium heat and stir until the mixture comes to the boil. Cook for 4–5 minutes, stirring from time to time, letting the mixture thicken and reduce.

3. Spoon into an ovenproof dish, smooth the surface, and spread the sweetcorn over the top.

4. Mix the cheese and breadcrumbs together and sprinkle over. Dot with a few knobs of butter, place in the oven and bake for 15 minutes until golden. Sprinkle with some chopped chives and serve at once.

Egg and Vegetable Nests

THERE are many variations on this theme. The one I give in detail is the most colourful but the others taste just as good. If you do not have time to cook the eggs in the oven they can be cooked on top of the stove. Simply break the eggs into the vegetables in the frying pan and cover with a lid. They will be cooked in about 5 minutes. In this case it is not necessary to moisten the yolks with fromage frais.

INGREDIENTS

200g (7oz) carrots, peeled
2 large leeks, approximately 250g (9oz), trimmed
1 bunch spring onions, trimmed
175g (6oz) mangetouts, trimmed

2 tablespoons cooking oil
4 eggs
fromage frais
salt and freshly ground black pepper

1. Set the oven to 200°C/400°F/Gas Mark 6 and grease a shallow oven-proof dish.

2. Cut the carrots into 7.5cm (3 inch) lengths and then into very thin sticks. Cut the rest of the vegetables in the same way.

3. Heat the oil in a large frying pan and stir-fry the carrots for 2–3 minutes. Add the rest of the vegetables and continue to stir-fry for another 2–3 minutes.

4. Spoon the stir-fried vegetables into the prepared dish, making 4 shallow depressions in the mixture. Break an egg into each depression and top with a spoonful of fromage frais.

5. Season and bake for 10 minutes until the eggs are just set but the yolks are still runny.

VARIATIONS

◆ Use carrots alone and flavour with freshly chopped tarragon.

◆ Use thinly sliced celery, sliced beans or spring greens instead of mangetouts.

Polenta Pie

THE secret of this recipe is to use ingredients which need little or no preparation before going into the pie and I have discovered a wonderful ready-made polenta which can be used straight from the pack. It comes in a large thick sausage shape. You simply unwrap it and slice or mash with a fork, depending upon the recipe you plan to make. You can, of course, make your own polenta from scratch but you must be sure to buy the quick-cook variety. Cans of ready-chopped tomatoes are ideal, too. Drain and keep the juice for use in soups and sauces.

This recipe is from the Val d'Aosta, and Fontina would be the cheese of choice. It is really creamy and melts easily and these are the characteristics needed. Alternatives include cream cheeses such as Philadelphia.

INGREDIENTS

1 × 400g (14oz) can chopped tomatoes
salt and freshly ground black pepper
675g (1½lb) ready-made polenta, sliced
   into 12 thick slices

grated nutmeg
4 sprigs of fresh basil
200g (7oz) Philadelphia cream cheese

1. Set the oven to 200°C/400°F/Gas Mark 6 and brush a shallow ovenproof dish with cooking oil.

2. Place the chopped tomatoes in a saucepan with the seasoning and bring to the boil.

3. Layer the slices of polenta in the prepared dish with the chopped tomatoes and slices of cheese, seasoning and scattering with nutmeg and basil as you go. Finish with a layer of tomato.

4. Place in the oven and bake for 20 minutes until bubbly. Serve at once.

VARIATION

♦ Top with a layer of grated Cheddar or Parmesan cheese.

CHAPTER SIX

Casseroles & Curries

CASSEROLES can be just as successful cooked on top of the stove as in the oven. These dishes do not need a long cooking time if you use a medium heat to keep the liquid on the boil and reduce it sufficiently to give a good flavour. Stir from time to time to make sure that the casserole does not stick to the base of the pan.

The recipes in this chapter are inspired by the cooking of Eastern Europe, Africa and the Far East. All these regions have a history of producing hearty vegetable dishes which go very well with boiled or steamed rice, noodles, couscous, cracked wheat and cornmeal.

There is also a recipe for Almond Casserole Dumplings. These can be added to casseroles such as Broccoli Hotpot, Coconut Bean Stew, Oriental Vegetable Casserole with Okra, and to Italian Braised Pumpkin in Chapter 9. If you are adding dumplings you may like to use slightly more stock.

Mushroom Goulash with Noodles

❖

THE best results are achieved with a mixture of medium-sized brown mushrooms and small closed cup mushrooms. However you can make this goulash with either one alone. Start the meal with Lemon Bean and Almond Salad (see page 46) and finish with fresh fruit.

INGREDIENTS
---

1 large leek, trimmed, cleaned and sliced

1 green pepper, seeded and chopped

3 tablespoons olive oil

2 tablespoons paprika

450g (1lb) closed cup mushrooms, thickly sliced

175g (6oz) brown mushrooms, thickly sliced

150ml (¼ pint) vegetable stock

3 tablespoons tomato purée

4 tablespoons freshly chopped parsley

salt and freshly ground black pepper

225g (½lb) flat noodles

3 tablespoons sour cream or puréed silken tofu

---

1. Gently fry the leek and green pepper in the oil for 2 minutes. Stir in the paprika and cook for another minute or so.

2. Stir in the mushrooms and cover. Cook gently for 5 minutes, stirring occasionally. Add the stock and the tomato purée, half the parsley and the seasoning. Cook, uncovered, for 10 minutes.

3. Cook the noodles in plenty of boiling salted water for about 8–10 minutes or for the length of time specified on the pack.

4. Stir the sour cream or tofu into the goulash and reheat. Drain the noodles very well and pile onto serving plates. Top with the goulash and garnish with the remaining parsley.

Coconut Bean Stew Ⓥ

T HIS African stew would probably be eaten with ugali (a thick corn-meal mush). The nearest European equivalent is polenta and I often serve it with this. Add a dish of wilted greens flavoured with cinnamon for a well-balanced meal.

INGREDIENTS

1 onion, peeled and chopped
1 clove garlic, peeled and chopped
1 green pepper, seeded and chopped
1 tablespoon cooking oil
2 teaspoons coriander seeds
1 teaspoon caraway seeds

1 small dried red chilli
1 tablespoon tomato purée
1 × 450g (1lb) can kidney beans, drained
  and washed
1 × 400ml (14fl oz) can coconut milk
2 tablespoons desiccated coconut

1. Fry the onion, garlic and pepper in the cooking oil for about 5 minutes until lightly browned.

2. Crush the coriander and caraway seeds with the chilli using a pestle and mortar or grind in an electric grinder. Stir into the vegetables and cook for another minute.

3. Add the tomato purée, kidney beans and coconut milk, and bring the mixture to the boil. Cook, uncovered, over a medium heat for 10–15 minutes until the sauce has thickened.

4. Divide between 4 plates, garnish with the coconut, and serve.

VARIATION

◆ If you do not like caraway, this dish is also very good made with ½ teaspoon fennel seeds and 5–6 whole allspice instead.

Oriental Vegetable Casserole with Okra

❖

THIS is another dish which is cooked in coconut milk but with the spicing of Southern India, rather than Africa, and the result is quite different. Serve with rice or noodles.

―――――――――――― INGREDIENTS ――――――――――――

2 large onions, peeled and coarsely
  chopped
2 large cloves garlic, peeled and chopped
2 teaspoons freshly grated root ginger
3 tablespoons cooking oil
2 teaspoons mild curry powder
3 carrots, peeled and cut into thick
  rounds
175g (6oz) baby sweetcorn

175g (6oz) green beans, trimmed and
  cut into 4cm (1½ inch) lengths
1 × 400ml (14fl oz) can coconut milk
75ml (3fl oz) vegetable stock
a small bunch of coriander, freshly
  chopped
salt and freshly ground black pepper
225g (½lb) fresh or frozen baby okra

◆

1. Gently fry the onion, garlic and ginger in the oil for 3–4 minutes to soften but not brown. Stir in the curry powder.

2. Add the carrots, sweetcorn, beans, coconut milk, stock, half the coriander, and the seasoning. Bring the mixture to the boil. Cook, uncovered, over a medium heat for about 15 minutes.

3. Add the okra and continue to boil for another 5 minutes until all the vegetables are tender and the sauce has thickened. Serve sprinkled with the remaining coriander.

Lentil and Vegetable Stew Ⓥ

❖

THE lentils give this colourful vegetable stew a thick velvety sauce. The original recipe (without the onions) came from the Gujarat area of India where much of the food is vegetarian. For a really authentic taste leave out the onions and spices and use Bart's Gujarat Masala Paste instead.

Serve with Eastern Fried Rice with Celeriac (see page 90) or Almond and Herb Rice (see page 92).

——————— INGREDIENTS ———————

2 tablespoons cooking oil
½ teaspoon whole cumin seeds
½ teaspoon fenugreek or black mustard
  seeds (optional)
1 onion, peeled and finely chopped
1 green chilli, seeded and finely chopped
1 tablespoon grated root ginger
1 teaspoon ground turmeric
115g (4oz) split red or yellow lentils

1 large carrot, approximately 175g (6oz),
  peeled and sliced into thin rounds
salt and freshly ground black pepper
200ml (8fl oz) vegetable stock
2 large courgettes or winter squash,
  approximately 300g (10oz), sliced into
  rounds
4 tomatoes, coarsely chopped

◆

1. Heat the oil in a large saucepan and fry the whole spices for 30 seconds. Add the onion, chilli, ginger and turmeric and fry for another 2–3 minutes. Stir in the lentils and make sure they are well coated with the spicy mixture.

2. Add the carrot, seasoning and vegetable stock and bring to the boil. Cook over a medium heat for 5–6 minutes.

3. Stir the mixture and add the courgettes or squash and tomatoes. Return to the boil, reduce the heat and simmer for 10–15 minutes until the carrots are tender. Serve at once.

Broccoli Hotpot Ⓥ

❖

Y OU should use large headed broccoli or calabrese for this recipe. Purple sprouting broccoli would not really work. Take care not to overcook the broccoli. It will easily be ready in 10 minutes if it is cut into small florets.

Serve with Almond Casserole Dumplings (see page 77), couscous or rice.

--------- INGREDIENTS ---------

1 large or 2 small leeks, trimmed, cleaned and sliced
1 large carrot, peeled and sliced into thin rounds
2 tablespoons cooking oil
1 teaspoon cornflour

200ml (8fl oz) vegetable stock
1 large potato, peeled and diced
½ teaspoon dried mixed herbs
salt and freshly ground black pepper
250g (9oz) head broccoli or calabrese, cut into small florets

♦

1. Gently fry the leeks and carrot in the cooking oil for 2–4 minutes.

2. Mix the cornflour with a little of the stock to make a cream and then stir in all the remaining stock. Add to the vegetables with the potato, mixed herbs and seasoning.

3. Stir well, then place the broccoli on top so that it will cook by steaming. Bring the mixture to the boil.

4. Cover and cook over a medium heat, stirring from time to time, for about 10 minutes until all the vegetables are cooked through and the sauce has thickened a little.

5. Just before serving, fold the broccoli carefully into the vegetable mixture. Serve at once.

Almond Casserole Dumplings

I VARY the flavourings in these simple dumplings depending on the dish they are to accompany. For example, I use toasted ground almonds for Broccoli Hotpot (see page 76) or ground cumin for Oriental Vegetable Casserole with Okra (see page 74).

The mixture also makes very good soup dumplings. Shape into smaller balls and flavour with freshly grated ginger for Thai Soup with Lemon Grass and Coriander (see page 25) or with grated lemon zest for Leek and Mustard Soup with Mushrooms (see page 34).

INGREDIENTS

25g (1oz) wholemeal breadcrumbs
2 tablespoons milk
25g (1oz) ground almonds
1 small egg (size 4), beaten
50g (2oz) self-raising flour
salt and freshly ground black pepper

OPTIONAL FLAVOURINGS
1 teaspoon ground cumin
1 tablespoon freshly grated root ginger
1 teaspoon grated lemon zest

◆

1. Soak the breadcrumbs in the milk for 5–6 minutes. Add the almonds and egg and beat together. Stir in the flour, seasoning and your chosen flavouring if desired.

2. Shape the mixture into 12 balls for casseroles and stews or about 16 balls for soup.

3. Drop all the dumplings into a large pan of boiling water, making sure that there is enough room for them to cook without touching each other too much.

4. Bring the water to the boil and simmer for 10–15 minutes, turning the dumplings from time to time. After about 12 minutes cut one of the dumplings in half to see if it is cooked through. If not, continue cooking for another 2–3 minutes until it is fluffy all the way through. When the dumplings are cooked lift them out with a slotted spoon and transfer to the casserole or soup.

Potato and Celery Stew

THIS is an easy all-in-one accompaniment to dishes such as grilled vegeburgers or tofu burgers, stuffed vegetables or nut roasts. If you are really in a hurry you can simply serve the stew as a meal for two, adding a large sprinkling of grated cheese.

INGREDIENTS

2 small onions, peeled and finely
  chopped
1 clove garlic, peeled and finely chopped
1 tablespoon cooking oil
4 large potatoes, peeled and sliced

4 large sticks celery, trimmed and sliced
115ml (4fl oz) vegetable stock
1 tablespoon freshly chopped dill
salt and freshly ground black pepper

1. Fry the onions and garlic in the cooking oil in a deep frying pan with a lid for 2–3 minutes to soften but not brown.

2. Add the potatoes and celery and continue to fry gently for a further 2–3 minutes, stirring from time to time.

3. Add all the remaining ingredients. Stir and bring to the boil. Cover and simmer for 15 minutes until the vegetables are tender. Serve at once.

VARIATIONS
◆ Use freshly chopped sage or tarragon in place of dill.

◆ Add a diced sweet and sour pickled cucumber to the mix for a more piquant flavour.

Mixed Root Vegetable Curry

❖

YOU can choose any combination of three or four different root vegetables in this simple curry from Northern India. However parsnips
give a very definite flavour so go easy on these. I used mooli, carrots and
swede in testing. To ensure that the dish cooks in time, cut the vegetables
into very small dice.

INGREDIENTS

2 tablespoons cooking oil
½ teaspoon cumin seeds
seeds from 4 cardamom pods
¼ teaspoon fennel seeds (optional)
1 large onion, peeled and minced or very
 · finely chopped
2 cloves garlic, peeled and crushed
1 tablespoon freshly grated root ginger
1 fresh green or red chilli, seeded and
 finely chopped

1kg (2lb 4oz) mixed root vegetables
 (carrots, celeriac, Jerusalem
 artichokes, mooli, parsnips, swede, or
 turnips), peeled and diced
1 large potato, peeled and diced
1 × 400ml (14fl oz) can tomato juice
salt and freshly ground black pepper
fried almonds or pinenuts

◆

1. Heat the oil in a deep heavy-based saucepan and fry the spices for
 about a minute. Remove from the heat if they start to smoke. Stir in
 the onion, garlic and ginger and continue frying for another 1–2 minutes.

2. Stir in the remaining ingredients, except the fried nuts, and bring the
 mixture to the boil. Cover and reduce the heat and cook for 15–20
 minutes, stirring from time to time.

3. Serve sprinkled with the fried nuts.

VARIATION

◆ Non-vegans might like to substitute yogurt or single cream for one-
third of the tomato juice. The cream, particularly, gives the dish a rich,
silky texture and flavour.

Pumpkin and Chickpea Couscous Ⓥ

❖

Couscous is very popular in North Africa where it is one of the staple foods. It is made of tiny pieces of semolina which are best steamed or cooked according to the quick method given below. Check the cooking instructions on the packet before you buy the couscous to see if it is suitable for this method.

This dish is traditionally served with a North African chilli sauce called harissa which you can now buy ready-made.

―――――――――― INGREDIENTS ――――――――――

salt
3–4 tablespoons olive oil
225g (½lb) couscous

SAUCE
2 teaspoons cumin seeds
2 teaspoons dried oregano
¼ teaspoon ground cinnamon
4 tablespoons cooking oil
2 large onions, peeled and coarsely
  chopped

2 large cloves garlic, peeled and chopped
2 whole fresh green or red chillies
200g (7oz) celery, trimmed and chopped
1 × 1.25kg (2lb 12oz) pumpkin, peeled,
  seeded and chopped
1 × 400g (14oz) can chickpeas
500ml (16fl oz) vegetable stock
salt and freshly ground black pepper
a little potato flour or cornflour (optional)

◆

1. To make the sauce, dry-fry the cumin seeds in a heavy-based saucepan until they begin to brown. Add the oregano and cinnamon and stir.

2. Next add the oil, onions and garlic and fry for 2–3 minutes until lightly browned. Add all the remaining sauce ingredients and bring to the boil. Cover and simmer for 15–20 minutes.

3. To make the couscous, place 250ml (9fl oz) water in a large heavy-based saucepan with some salt and 1 tablespoon olive oil. Bring to the boil. Remove from the heat and stir in the couscous. Leave to stand for 3 minutes.

4. Return the pan to the heat and stir in the rest of the olive oil. Cook over a low heat for another 3 minutes. You will need to stir all the time to prevent the couscous sticking to the base of the pan. After 3 min-

utes turn off the heat and cover with a lid. Leave to stand until required.

5. If you do not like a very runny sauce, thicken with a little potato flour or cornflour dissolved in a little water. Stir in and bring to the boil. Cook for 1 minute and serve over the couscous.

Curried Green Bananas with Eggs

THE easiest way to make this dish is to buy dessert bananas while they are still green. These are not difficult to find, as most fruit coming into the supermarket is unripe! Of course, if you live near a West Indian community you should be able to find the real thing. If you cannot find any kind of green bananas you can use ordinary bananas but you will need to reduce the cooking time by at least half.

If you prefer to leave out the eggs you can serve the curry with boiled rice and another curry or with a vegetable dish from Chapter 9.

INGREDIENTS

½ teaspoon cumin seeds
1 tablespoon cooking oil
1 tablespoon curry powder
4 unripe green bananas, peeled and
   sliced

115ml (4fl oz) canned coconut milk
salt and freshly ground black pepper
2 eggs, beaten

1. Fry the cumin seeds in the oil for about a minute, then stir in the curry powder and the sliced bananas. When the bananas are well coated, pour in the coconut milk and add the seasoning.

2. Bring to the boil and simmer, uncovered, for about 20 minutes until the bananas are tender and the liquid has thickened. Stir in the beaten egg and serve.

Sag Aloo with Greens

❖

IN AN Indian restaurant *sag* usually means 'spinach' but it can also be translated as 'greens'. This recipe could include cabbage, kale and spring or Eastern greens, as well as the more usual spinach.

Serve with Curried Green Bananas (see page 81), with or without the eggs according to taste, some chapatis and plain or lightly spiced yogurt with cucumber.

————————— INGREDIENTS —————————

1 tablespoon cooking oil
½ teaspoon mustard or cumin seeds
1 large clove garlic, peeled and chopped
1 small onion, peeled and minced or very finely chopped
1 teaspoon ground coriander
1 teaspoon ground turmeric

¼ teaspoon chilli powder
2 medium-sized potatoes, peeled and diced
200g (7oz) greens, finely shredded
115ml (4fl oz) vegetable stock
250g (9oz) frozen chopped spinach

◆

1. Heat the cooking oil in a pan and fry the mustard or cumin seeds for 30 seconds. Add the garlic and onion and continue frying for another 2–3 minutes.

2. Stir in the spices and then the potatoes, making sure that the potatoes are well covered with the spicy mixture. Add the greens and stock and bring to the boil. Cover and cook for about 10 minutes until the vegetables are almost tender.

3. Meanwhile remove the spinach from the freezer and place in a small saucepan to thaw over a low heat. Stir from time to time.

4. When the vegetables are almost cooked add the spinach and return to the boil. Reduce the heat and simmer for a further 5 minutes until the vegetables are fully cooked.

Curried Chestnuts

❖

IT IS now possible to buy peeled and cooked chestnuts in cans and in vacuum packs. Either way they keep for a considerable time in the storecupboard. The chestnuts are unsweetened and ready to use.

This unusually sweet curry is very filling and you only need a small quantity. Serve with Mixed Root Vegetable Curry (see page 79) and boiled rice.

INGREDIENTS

1 onion, peeled and finely chopped
1 carrot, peeled and finely chopped
1 clove garlic, peeled and crushed
   (optional)
1 tablespoon cooking oil
1 teaspoon flour

1 teaspoon curry powder
200g (7oz) peeled and cooked chestnuts
25g (1oz) raisins
1 tablespoon mango chutney
1 tablespoon vinegar

◆

1. Fry the onion and carrot, and garlic if using, in the oil until lightly browned. Stir in the flour and curry powder and cook for another minute or so.

2. Gradually add 300ml (½ pint) water, stirring all the time, and bring the mixture to the boil. Reduce the heat and add all the remaining ingredients.

3. Cover and simmer for 15 minutes until the vegetables are cooked through.

Gujarati-Style Cauliflower

❖

MANY people from Gujarat do not eat onion or garlic – often considered to be essential ingredients in Indian cooking – so this recipe uses neither. Instead, it relies on tamarind, mustard seed, chilli and coconut for its flavour.

It is possible to find tamarind in specialist ethnic shops but I use a proprietary Tamarind and Date Chutney which gives a very similar effect, particularly as the original recipe used quite a lot of brown sugar.

Mustard seed is much easier to find than tamarind. It is usually on sale in supermarket spice racks. Go easy on this and the chilli if you do not like dishes too hot, as the chutney also contains them both.

――――――――――― INGREDIENTS ―――――――――――

1 tablespoon Tamarind and Date
  Chutney
2 tablespoons cooking oil
1 teaspoon mustard seeds
1 cauliflower, broken into small florets

1 teaspoon ground turmeric
¼ teaspoon chilli powder
salt
2 tablespoons desiccated coconut

◆

1. Mix the chutney with 115ml (4fl oz) water and keep on one side.

2. Heat the oil in a pan and fry the mustard seeds. Cover the pan with a lid while you do this or the seeds will pop out. Stop frying after a maximum of a minute or the seeds will burn. Add the cauliflower and continue frying.

3. Add the chutney and water mixture and all the remaining ingredients and bring to the boil. Continue cooking over a low heat for 15 minutes until the cauliflower is just tender. Stir once or twice during this time.

4. If there is any liquid left in the bottom of the pan, quickly boil it off.

CHAPTER SEVEN

Filling Food

This chapter includes a range of recipes for filling foods like noodles, rice, cracked wheat and potatoes. Here again the inspiration for these dishes comes from around the world. There are ideas from Central Europe, Southern India, China, Mexico and the Middle East.

Most of the recipes specify the kind of noodles or rice to use but there is no reason why you should not substitute other types. The choice of noodles is particularly wide, taking in fresh and dried Italian pasta, Chinese dried egg noodles and rice noodles and a variety of Japanese noodles such as rye and buckwheat.

I usually use long-grain rice for savoury cooking and my favourite is Basmati. Brown rice can also be used, but remember that it may need a little more water and it will take longer to cook than white rice.

The rice dishes and some of the potato dishes can be served with stews and casseroles from Chapter 6 or, indeed, with any of the main course recipes.

Others, like Noodles with Chickpeas, Tofu and Coconut, Vegetable Noodles with Nut Sauce, Cracked Wheat with Okra, or Potato, Sweetcorn and Spinach Cake, only need the addition of a salad to turn them into a full main course in their own right.

Noodles with Chickpeas, Tofu and Coconut

❖

I WAS given this unusual recipe by a family friend who spends a good deal of time in Southern India. She is not sure of the exact origins of the dish as it seems to have been handed down from cook to cook, each one subtracting or adding an ingredient depending on what was available. You can treat it in just the same way, adding cumin or ginger and subtracting chilli or coriander as the mood takes you.

─────────── INGREDIENTS ───────────

25g (1oz) desiccated coconut
1 × 400g (14oz) can chickpeas, drained
1 × 300g (10oz) block plain tofu
1 large clove garlic, peeled and crushed
1 fresh red chilli, seeded and chopped
2 tablespoons freshly chopped coriander
2 tablespoons dark soy sauce

freshly ground black pepper
2 tablespoons cooking oil
250g (9oz) Chinese dried egg noodles
1 bunch spring onions, trimmed and
    sliced on the slant
¼ teaspoon dried mixed herbs
salt and freshly ground black pepper

◆

1. Toast the coconut under the grill or in a dry frying pan until lightly browned, taking care not to burn it. Set aside.

2. Mash or grind the chickpeas and tofu together and stir in the garlic, chilli, coriander, soy sauce and black pepper.

3. Heat the oil in a frying pan and spoon in the chickpea and tofu mixture. Press down to form a large cake and fry for 3–4 minutes until well browned. Turn over in sections and cook on the other side for another 4–5 minutes.

4. Cook the noodles as directed on the pack. Drain well and toss with the spring onions, herbs and seasoning.

5. The chickpea and tofu mixture will be fairly crumbly and should simply be scattered over the prepared noodles. Top with the toasted coconut.

Vegetable Noodles with Nut Sauce

❖

PEANUT butter is the obvious choice for this recipe but there are some other nut butters available in healthfood and delicatessen shops. Look out for cashew, walnut or almond butter. You can also use tahini (sesame paste). Each one will give the dish a slightly different flavour.

This recipe works well with any kind of noodles: choose from Chinese egg or rice noodles, Japanese buckwheat noodles or Italian pasta.

INGREDIENTS

250g (9oz) noodles
salt
4 tablespoons cooking oil
1 onion, peeled and finely chopped
2 tablespoons nut butter
3 tablespoons orange juice
115ml (4fl oz) vegetable stock

½ teaspoon whole coriander seeds
225g (½lb) carrots, peeled and coarsely grated
175g (6oz) celeriac, kohlrabi or parsnips, peeled and coarsely grated
1 teaspoon grated orange zest
1–2 tablespoons soy sauce

---

1. Cook the noodles in lightly salted water, as directed on the pack.

2. Heat half the oil in a saucepan and fry the onion for about 2 minutes to soften. Stir in the nut butter and orange juice and gradually stir in the stock to give a smooth paste. Heat the mixture through, taking care not to overcook it or it will thicken up. If this does happen simply add more stock. Set aside.

3. Heat the remaining oil in a wok or deep frying pan and fry the coriander seeds for a minute until they start to pop. Add the grated vegetables and stir-fry for 1–2 minutes.

4. Drain the noodles and add to the vegetables. Toss well together over a high heat. Add the orange zest and soy sauce and spoon onto 4 plates. Top with the nut sauce and serve at once.

Warm Spicy Noodle Salad

❖

CHINESE thread egg noodles are the best choice for this dish but you can use any kind of quick-cook egg noodles. Serve with Tofu Sesame Slices (see page 40) or Oriental Sweetcorn Fritters (see page 39).

—————— INGREDIENTS ——————

1 × 300g (10oz) pack dried Chinese thread egg noodles
1 large green pepper, seeded
1 large bunch spring onions, trimmed
1 × 225g (½lb) can water chestnuts, drained
2–3 tablespoons light soy sauce

2 teaspoons roasted sesame oil
juice of ½ lemon
1 tablespoon sake or dry sherry (optional)
½ teaspoon freshly grated root ginger
freshly ground black pepper

◆

1. Place the noodles in a bowl and cover with boiling water. Leave to stand for the time directed on the pack (usually 5–8 minutes).

2. Thinly shred the green pepper, thinly slice the spring onions on the slant, and slice the water chestnuts. Keep on one side.

3. Beat 2 tablespoons soy sauce with the roasted sesame oil, lemon juice, sake or sherry if using, grated root ginger and pepper.

4. Drain the noodles very well and toss first with the prepared vegetables and then with the soy sauce mixture. Leave to stand for 5 minutes.

5. Taste the noodles to see if they need any more seasoning. If they do, add a little soy sauce. Serve at once.

VARIATION

◆ If you are not serving this salad with the tofu slices, garnish with a few sprigs of fresh coriander.

Six Jewel Rice

❖

THE six jewels are, of course, the vegetables, which give the colour to this attractive rice dish. If you do not have exactly these vegetables use whatever you have to hand or simply make five or even four jewel rice!

INGREDIENTS

1 red pepper, seeded and diced
1 small carrot, peeled and very finely diced
2 small courgettes, diced
50g (2oz) frozen sweetcorn
50g (2oz) frozen peas

100g (3½oz) mushrooms, diced
225g (½lb) long-grain rice
¼ teaspoon dried mixed herbs
celery salt (optional)
freshly ground black pepper
450ml (16fl oz) boiling vegetable stock

◆

1. Mix all the vegetables with the rice, herbs and seasoning. Place in a large saucepan and cover with the boiling vegetable stock.

2. Stir once and bring back to the boil. Cover, reduce the heat and simmer for 15 minutes. Check to see if all the liquid has been absorbed. If not, cook for a further 5 minutes.

3. Leave to stand for 1–2 minutes, then fluff up with a fork and serve.

VARIATION
◆ Top with scrambled eggs and spring onion flowers, or crumbled smoked tofu and freshly chopped herbs, to turn this into a nutritious main course.

Eastern Fried Rice with Celeriac

❖

YOU can use any root vegetable in this unusual rice dish which was inspired by an old recipe I came across in my mother's scrap book many years ago. I have tried it with parsnips, carrots and mooli and they all work very well.

── INGREDIENTS ──

200g (7oz) long-grain rice
1 small onion, peeled and finely chopped
1 stick celery, trimmed and finely
  chopped
2 tablespoons toasted pinenuts
salt and freshly ground black pepper
2 tablespoons cooking oil

225g (½lb) celeriac, peeled and cut into
  thin sticks
2 cloves garlic, peeled and crushed
3 tablespoons freshly chopped coriander
grated rind of ½ lemon
¼ teaspoon minced chilli in oil or a few
  drops of Tabasco

1. Put 400ml (14fl oz) water in a saucepan and bring to the boil. Mix the rice, onion, celery, pinenuts and seasoning together and spoon into the saucepan of boiling water. Return the mixture to the boil, stir again and cover. Reduce the heat and simmer for 12–15 minutes until all the liquid has been absorbed and the rice is tender.

2. Heat the oil in a wok or deep frying pan and add the sticks of celeriac. Stir-fry for 2–3 minutes.

3. Prepare all the remaining ingredients and mix together in a cup. Keep on one side.

4. Add the cooked rice to the celeriac in the pan and stir-fry for another minute or so. Now add the garlic mixture, continue to stir-fry over a medium heat for another 2–3 minutes, and serve.

Rice with Sweetcorn

❖

THIS Mexican dish has a good flavour of its own and it makes an excellent main course with Leek and Horseradish Salad (see page 128). It can also be served with any kind of casserole or with stuffed or grilled vegetables. You can vary the amount of chilli to suit your own palate or to go with your chosen accompaniment.

INGREDIENTS

1 small onion, peeled and finely chopped
2 cloves garlic, peeled and crushed
1 tablespoon cooking oil
225g (½lb) long-grain rice
1 green pepper, seeded and chopped

2 green chillies, seeded and finely chopped
175g (6oz) sweetcorn
450ml (16fl oz) vegetable stock
salt and freshly ground black pepper

◆

1. Fry the onion and garlic in the cooking oil over a medium heat for 3–4 minutes until lightly browned. Add the rice and stir well.

2. Now add all the remaining ingredients and bring to the boil. Stir and cover. Reduce the heat and cook for 15 minutes.

3. Check to see that all the liquid has been taken up and that the rice is cooked. Fluff up with a fork and serve at once.

VARIATIONS

◆ Stir in 4 or 5 finely chopped spring onions just before serving.

◆ Sprinkle with some toasted nuts if you want to add extra protein to the meal.

Almond and Herb Rice

❖

THIS is quite delicious enough to eat on its own with a simple green salad. However it also makes a very good accompaniment for most of the casseroles and curries in Chapter 6.

INGREDIENTS

75g (3oz) ground almonds
550ml (18fl oz) vegetable stock
1 clove garlic, peeled and crushed
juice of ½ lemon
a few drops of Tabasco to taste

225g (½lb) Basmati rice
salt and freshly ground black pepper
3 tablespoons freshly chopped parsley
1 tablespoon freshly chopped chervil

1. Mix the ground almonds with the stock and bring to the boil. Add the garlic, lemon juice and Tabasco and simmer for 10 minutes.

2. Pour in the rice. Return the mixture to the boil and stir once. Cover, reduce the heat and simmer for 15 minutes until all the liquid has been absorbed and the rice is tender.

3. Fluff up with a fork, season to taste and stir in the fresh herbs. Serve at once.

VARIATION
♦ Use mint instead of chervil and cut back on the garlic.

Cracked Wheat with Okra

❖

YOU can use either fresh or frozen okra for this Middle Eastern dish. Either way, choose very small or baby okra. You can find the latter in the frozen food compartments of some supermarkets.

This is another filling dish which is delicious on its own with a simple side salad. It also goes very well with most of the casseroles in Chapter 6.

INGREDIENTS

200g (7oz) cracked or bulgur wheat
250g (9oz) baby or very small okra
3 tablespoons olive oil
1 large onion, peeled and finely chopped
1 large red pepper, seeded and finely chopped

2 tomatoes, skinned and chopped
4 tablespoons white wine or vegetable stock
salt and freshly ground black pepper
6–8 sprigs of fresh coriander

---

1. Place the cracked wheat in a bowl and cover with boiling water. Leave to stand for at least 10 minutes. It should swell and take up most of the water.

2. Place the okra in a saucepan and cover with boiling water. Return to the boil and simmer for 3–4 minutes to soften.

3. Heat the olive oil in a frying pan and fry the onion and pepper for 2–3 minutes. Add the tomatoes and wine or stock and continue to cook for a further 3–4 minutes, stirring from time to time.

4. Drain the okra and the cracked wheat and dry them both on kitchen paper. Add to the onion and pepper mixture. Season well and cook over a high heat for 5–6 minutes, turning the mixture when it begins to brown on the base.

5. Serve garnished with the sprigs of fresh coriander.

Grated Potato Cakes

Serve these variations on Jewish *latkes* with one of the dishes in Chapter 6 or eat them as a tasty snack on their own with a little apple sauce.

--- INGREDIENTS ---

½ small onion, peeled
600g (1lb 5oz) potatoes, peeled
2 large eggs, beaten
3 tablespoons plain flour

salt and freshly ground black pepper
4 tablespoons freshly chopped dill
4 tablespoons cooking oil

1. Grate the onion into a large bowl and then grate in the potatoes. Mix with the eggs as quickly as possible to stop the potato discolouring. Stir in the remaining ingredients except the cooking oil.

2. Heat the cooking oil in a large frying pan. Drop 8 spoonfuls of the mixture into the hot oil and spread out so that they are fairly thin. Thicker cakes will take longer to cook.

3. Cook over a medium heat for 8–10 minutes on each side. They should be well browned on the outside and soft in the middle.

VARIATION

◆ For a completely different flavour use 2 tablespoons mustard and 1 tablespoon creamed horseradish in place of the dill.

Indian Mashed Potato Ⓥ

THIS simple dish has such a wonderfully aromatic flavour that it always disappears very fast! I love to eat it on its own, but it goes well with all the curried dishes in Chapter 6 and with Oriental Sweetcorn Fritters (see page 39).

The mixture also makes a very good stuffing for cabbage leaves and red peppers. Cook the leaves or peppers at the same time as the potatoes, then put the two together and steam for about 5 minutes before serving.

INGREDIENTS

675g (1½lb) potatoes, peeled and diced
salt
2 tablespoons cooking oil
1 teaspoon cumin seeds
1 green or red chilli, seeded and finely chopped

1 onion, peeled and finely chopped
1 teaspoon curry powder
1 tablespoon mango chutney, chopped
2 tablespoons freshly chopped coriander
salt and freshly ground black pepper

1. Steam the potatoes over boiling water for 5–8 minutes, depending on the size of the dice. Take care not to overcook them.

2. While the potatoes are cooking heat the oil in a saucepan and fry the cumin seeds for about a minute. Add the chilli and onion and fry for about 5 minutes until well browned. Stir in the curry powder, mango chutney, coriander and seasoning.

3. When the potatoes are cooked mash with a fork and stir in the spicy onion mixture. Spoon into a pudding basin and cover with clingfilm. Place in a pan with 2.5cm (1 inch) boiling water in the base and simmer for 5 minutes.

Potato, Sweetcorn and Spinach Cake

❖

THIS substantial vegetable cake can be served on its own with a tomato and onion salad. Alternatively it can be served with another dish such as Hard-Boiled Eggs in Onion Sauce (see page 100) or Stuffed Marrow Rings with Aubergines and Tomatoes (see page 103).

INGREDIENTS

4 medium to large potatoes
200g (7oz) celery (2 large sticks), cut into
   7.5cm (3 inch) lengths

350g (12oz) fresh leaf spinach, washed
salt and freshly ground black pepper
3–4 tablespoons extra virgin olive oil

---

1. Put the potatoes in their skins and the pieces of celery in a pan of boiling water and boil for 5–6 minutes. Peel the potatoes and dice finely. Chop the celery.

2. Drain the spinach and cook in a large saucepan over a low heat with no water at all. Remove from the heat as soon as the leaves wilt. Drain off as much water as possible by pressing the leaves down in a sieve. Coarsely chop with a knife.

3. Mix all the vegetables in a large bowl and season well.

4. Heat all the oil in a deep frying pan. Pour half the oil over the vegetables and toss together. Spoon the mixture into the frying pan and cook over a medium heat for 5–6 minutes until the base is well browned.

5. Put a plate over the pan and turn the vegetable cake onto it. Slide back into the pan to cook the second side. It will take another 5–6 minutes to brown.

6. Slide onto another warm plate to serve.

VARIATION

◆ Non-vegans might like to use 50–75g (2–3oz) butter in place of the oil. The butter gives a quite different flavour to the dish. You can also sprinkle it with grated smoked cheese just before serving.

Supper Dishes

THE recipes in this chapter are for quick dishes which can be served on their own or with bread to make a good simple meal. Other recipes use pasta or noodles to make an all-in-one supper or speedy lunch. Start in the American style with a green tossed salad and finish with a fresh or dried fruit platter.

Quite a few of the dishes are based on eggs or cheese but there are three or four recipes, such as Orange Stir-Fry Vegetables with Tofu, Stuffed Marrow Rings with Aubergines and Tomatoes, Polenta Slices with Devilled Mushrooms, and Pasta Shells with Fresh Beans and Tomato Sauce, which are suitable for vegans.

Quick Pan Haggarty with Sage

THIS is my mother's version of the old Northumbrian dish. She loved the combination of onions and sage and this mixture crops up in a number of her favourite recipes.

You can, of course, use left-over boiled potatoes and this speeds things up even more. In fact I have been known to cook too many potatoes just to make this dish the next day!

INGREDIENTS

1kg (2lb 4oz) or 4 large potatoes, peeled and sliced fairly thickly
salt
675g (1½lb) onions, peeled and sliced
1 tablespoon cooking oil

2 teaspoons dried sage
25g (1oz) butter or margarine
175g (6oz) mature Cheddar or hard goat's cheese, grated
salt and freshly ground black pepper

---

1. Place the potatoes in a pan and cover with boiling salted water. Cook over a medium heat for 8 minutes until almost, but not quite, soft. Drain very well and dry on kitchen paper.

2. Set the grill to high.

3. Fry the onions in the cooking oil until just starting to brown. This will take 5–6 minutes over a medium heat. Mix with the sage.

4. Melt the butter or margarine in another frying pan and layer the cooked potatoes with the onions and grated cheese, seasoning as you go. Cover and cook over a low to medium heat for about 10 minutes until well browned on the base.

5. Finish the top off under the grill.

VARIATION
♦ Add a layer of peeled and sliced tomatoes in the middle of the dish.

Egg and Cabbage Parcels

I N THIS recipe it is important to cook the cabbage leaves fully before scrambling the eggs, as they are not cooked again. The filling is put into the cooked leaves and the dish is served at once.

INGREDIENTS

8 cabbage or spring green leaves
450g (1lb) carrots, peeled and grated
4 eggs

a knob of butter
2 teaspoons dried tarragon
salt and freshly ground black pepper

---

1. Steam the cabbage or spring green leaves in a steamer for 15–20 minutes until tender.

2. Place the carrots in a small saucepan and cover with boiling water. Return to the boil and simmer for 5–6 minutes until the carrot is soft. Drain, retaining the carrot water for stock.

3. When the cabbage leaves are cooked, melt the butter in a saucepan and scramble the eggs with 2 tablespoons cold water until lightly set. Mix with the cooked carrot, tarragon and seasoning.

4. Place a spoonful of this mixture in the centre of each cooked cabbage leaf and fold up into a parcel. Serve at once.

VARIATION
◆ Use kohlrabi and mint, or parsnips and sage, in place of carrot and tarragon.

Hard-Boiled Eggs in Onion Sauce

I USUALLY serve this old French dish with plenty of crisp baguette but you could accompany it with boiled potatoes or large ribbon noodles tossed in butter and herbs.

In the original recipe the onion sauce is rubbed through a sieve or, in today's terms, puréed in a blender. However I rather like the texture of the onions in the sauce and I do not usually bother to purée it.

INGREDIENTS

6 large eggs
50g (2oz) butter
450g (1lb) onions, peeled and chopped
50g (2oz) plain flour
600ml (1 pint) hot milk

1 tablespoon freshly chopped or
   1 teaspoon dried tarragon
a pinch of dried thyme
salt and freshly ground black pepper

1. Cook the eggs in boiling water for 12 minutes to hard-boil.

2. Melt the butter in a saucepan and add the onions. Cook very gently over a very low heat for 8–10 minutes until the onions are soft. Do not allow them to brown.

3. Stir in the flour and blend well. Gradually add the hot milk and bring to the boil. Simmer for 3–4 minutes and add the herbs and seasoning.

4. Peel and slice or roughly chop the eggs and layer in a warmed heat-proof dish with the sauce. Serve at once.

VARIATION

◆ Top the dish with 50g (2oz) Gruyère or Emmental cheese mixed with 25g (1oz) fresh breadcrumbs, and brown under a hot grill.

Belgian Braised Chicory with Eggs

THIS dish is based on the small compact vegetable which we call chicory but which the Belgians actually call endive!

It is quite easy to omit the eggs if you are vegan or cutting back on your cholesterol intake. You could use slices of fried tofu in their place and replace the butter with soya margarine.

INGREDIENTS

4 long slim heads Belgian chicory
1 tablespoon cooking oil
1 large onion, peeled and finely sliced
25g (1oz) butter
2 large potatoes, peeled and finely diced
150ml (¼ pint) vegetable stock

2 tablespoons lemon juice
2 teaspoons light soy sauce
2 tablespoons freshly chopped or
   1 teaspoon dried tarragon
salt and freshly ground black pepper
4 eggs

1. Trim any bruised leaves from the outside of the chicory and cut a triangular-shaped core from the base of each head, as this is where the bitterness lies. If the chicory is very bulbous cut it in half lengthways.

2. Heat the oil in a large saucepan and fry the onion until golden brown. Add the butter and prepared chicory and toss over a medium heat for a minute or so. Add the potatoes and shake the pan well to coat the vegetables with the onion and fat.

3. Add all the remaining ingredients except the eggs and bring to the boil. Cover and simmer for 20 minutes, stirring from time to time.

4. Fry the eggs in a little more oil. Spoon one head of chicory onto each plate and share out the potatoes. Top each portion with a fried egg and serve at once.

Orange Stir-Fry Vegetables with Tofu

❖

THE orange goes extremely well with both the cauliflower and the leeks in this easy-to-prepare and very versatile dish. The tofu, of course, takes up all the flavours. Serve with Chinese egg noodles, rice, couscous or bulgur wheat.

——————————— INGREDIENTS ———————————

juice and grated zest of 2 oranges
300g (10oz) block tofu, diced
2 tablespoons tahini
4 tablespoons vegetable stock
2 tablespoons light soy sauce
2 tablespoons cooking oil
2.5cm (1 inch) fresh root ginger, peeled and cut into thin sticks

1 bunch spring onions, trimmed and sliced on the slant
1 small head cauliflower, cut into florets
1 red pepper, seeded and sliced
2 large leeks, trimmed and thinly sliced
salt and freshly ground black pepper

◆

1. Sprinkle the orange zest over the diced tofu and keep on one side until required.

2. Spoon the tahini into a cup and gradually stir in the stock and then the soy sauce. Keep on one side with the orange juice.

3. Heat half the oil in a wok or deep frying pan and stir-fry the ginger and spring onions for 1 minute. Add the cauliflower and pepper and stir-fry for 2–3 minutes. Add the leeks and cook for another 1–2 minutes.

4. Pour on the orange juice and bring to the boil. Simmer for 1–2 minutes until the vegetables are cooked to your liking. Add the tofu and orange zest and toss together.

5. Finally, when the tofu is heated through, add the tahini mixture. Season and stir over a medium heat until the sauce thickens. This will happen quite quickly. Spoon onto the prepared accompaniment at once.

6. Place the noodles or rice of your choice on 4 plates, top with the stir-fried tofu and vegetables, and serve.

Stuffed Marrow Rings
with Aubergines and Tomatoes

❖❖❖

THIS method of cooking marrow is very quick and you do not need to use the oven. However you have to keep your eye on it, as the marrow can very easily overcook and go soggy. I like to catch it when it still has a slight bite to it.

INGREDIENTS

1 large marrow, about 1kg (2lb 2oz) in weight
salt
1 large aubergine
3 tablespoons olive oil
2 large tomatoes, skinned and thickly sliced

STUFFING
2 onions, peeled and finely chopped
2 large carrots, peeled and grated
115ml (4fl oz) vegetable stock
115g (4oz) toasted pinenuts
4–6 olives, stoned and chopped
2–3 large sprigs of basil, chopped
salt and freshly ground black pepper

---

1. Cut the marrow into 8 thick slices and scoop out the seeds. Plunge the marrow rings into boiling salted water and cook for about 10 minutes until just tender.

2. Trim the ends off the aubergine and cut into 8 thick slices. Brush with oil and place under a hot grill. Cook for 2–3 minutes until lightly browned and turn over. Brush again with oil and cook for another 2–3 minutes.

3. To make the stuffing, fry the onions in the remaining oil until lightly browned. Add the carrots and stock and continue cooking for 5–6 minutes until the carrots are soft. Stir from time to time. Then add all the other stuffing ingredients and mix well together.

4. Drain the cooked marrow and dry on kitchen paper. Place one marrow ring on each slice of grilled aubergine. Fill each cavity with the stuffing mixture and top with a slice of tomato.

5. Drizzle with more oil and return to the grill. Cook for 3–4 minutes and serve at once.

Polenta Slices with Devilled Mushrooms

❖

READY-MADE polenta (see page 70) is ideal for this quick and very tasty snack. You can also serve the mushrooms on toast but the crisp yet moist polenta slices seem to work particularly well.

INGREDIENTS
---

1 large onion, peeled and thinly sliced
6 tablespoons olive oil
350g (12oz) small button mushrooms, sliced
1 heaped tablespoon mild mustard
1 tablespoon soy sauce

1 teaspoon paprika
¼ teaspoon dried thyme
salt and freshly ground black pepper
500g (1lb 2oz) ready-made polenta, cut into slices about 1cm (½ inch) thick
some freshly chopped parsley

◆

1. Fry the onion in 4 tablespoons olive oil over a medium heat for 3–4 minutes until it begins to brown. Add the mushrooms, reduce the heat and continue to fry gently for a further 3–4 minutes.

2. Stir in all the remaining ingredients, except the polenta and parsley, and bring to the boil. Simmer gently for 5–6 minutes while you cook the polenta.

3. Heat the remaining oil in another frying pan and fry the slices of polenta for about 3 minutes on each side until lightly browned.

4. Place the slices of polenta on serving plates. Boil off any excess liquid from the mushrooms and spoon over the polenta slices. Garnish with the parsley and serve at once.

Potato Tortilla with Creamed Spinach

I HAVE been making this simple potato tortilla for very many years now and it is still a favourite with all the family. I make no apology for the fact that it appeared in my very first vegetarian cookbook (though in none since) because I hope that a new generation of cooks will enjoy it as much as we do!

―――――――――― INGREDIENTS ――――――――――

750g (1lb 10oz) old potatoes, peeled and grated

1 large onion, peeled and very finely chopped

3 eggs, beaten

1 tablespoon plain flour

½ teaspoon dried mixed herbs

salt and freshly ground black pepper

2 tablespoons cooking oil

CREAMED SPINACH

450g (1lb) frozen chopped spinach

115g (4oz) full-fat cream cheese

6 tablespoons double cream

a pinch of grated nutmeg

salt and freshly ground black pepper

1. Strain any liquid from the grated potatoes and mix with the chopped onion, eggs, flour, mixed herbs and seasoning.

2. Heat the cooking oil in a non-stick frying pan and spoon in the potato and onion mixture. Spread out evenly over the base of the pan. Cook over a medium heat for 10–15 minutes, depending on the thickness of the tortilla.

3. When the base is well browned, turn over the tortilla and cook the other side for the same length of time.

4. Meanwhile, put the spinach in a saucepan and thaw over a low heat. Add the cheese, cut into small pieces, and the cream. Stir until all the cheese has melted and mixed into the spinach. Add the nutmeg and seasoning and bring to the boil.

5. Turn the tortilla out onto an oval serving plate and spoon the creamed spinach on to either end of the dish. Serve the tortilla cut into wedges with a dollop of spinach to accompany each portion.

Asparagus and Sweetcorn Omelette

FOR quick cooking use the largest frying pan you have. This allows all the ingredients to spread out into a set omelette about 5mm–1cm (¼–½ inch) thick. If you use a smaller pan it will take longer to cook.

INGREDIENTS

2 large potatoes, peeled and cut into
  chunks
2 medium-sized onions, peeled and
  thinly sliced
2 tablespoons cooking oil

225g (½lb) cooked or canned sweetcorn
1 × 415g (14½oz) can chopped
  asparagus spears, drained
6 eggs
salt and freshly ground black pepper

---

1. Set the grill to high.

2. Cook the potatoes in boiling water for about 10 minutes until just tender. Drain and dice.

3. Fry the onions in the oil for 3–4 minutes until lightly browned. Add the sweetcorn, asparagus spears and diced potato.

4. Beat the eggs with the seasoning and pour over the vegetables. Cook over a medium heat for about 5 minutes until the base is well browned. Finish off under a hot grill. Serve as soon as the top has set.

VARIATION

◆ Top with a little grated cheese before the omelette goes under the grill.

Broccoli Pesto Sauce with Tagliolini

I AM indebted to Bert Greene and his book *Greene on Greens* for the idea of using broccoli florets in this way though I have found that I prefer to use a slightly different balance of the other ingredients to that given in his book. Here is my version.

You can save the stalks from the broccoli and use them in any of the mixed vegetable casseroles or curries in Chapter 6.

INGREDIENTS

225g (½lb) dried tagliolini or long thin
   flat pasta
salt
200ml (8fl oz) olive oil
350g (12oz) broccoli
4 large sprigs of fresh basil

1 large clove garlic, peeled and chopped
75g (3oz) pinenuts
75g (3oz) freshly grated Parmesan
   cheese
salt and freshly ground black pepper

1. Cook the pasta in plenty of salted boiling water with 1 tablespoon of olive oil for the time directed on the pack. When the pasta reaches the *al dente* stage, drain it very well and toss in a little more oil.

2. Remove and discard the stalks from the broccoli and place the heads in a blender or food processor with the basil, garlic and pinenuts. Blend or process until smooth.

3. Stir in the rest of the oil and the cheese. Season, spoon over the drained pasta and serve at once.

Ravioli with Sage and Courgettes

THIS simple Roman recipe makes an excellent supper dish served with crusty bread and lashings of grated Parmesan cheese. Do try and buy the best Parmesan cheese you can find and grate it at home as required.

INGREDIENTS

450g (1lb) courgettes, thinly sliced
25g (1oz) butter
450g (1lb) fresh spinach and ricotta
   ravioli
salt

75ml (3fl oz) single cream
a few sprigs of fresh sage
freshly ground black pepper
115g (4oz) freshly grated Parmesan
   cheese

---

1. Gently fry the sliced courgettes in the butter to soften, but do not allow them to brown. This will take 5–6 minutes.

2. Cook the ravioli in plenty of boiling salted water for 3–5 minutes, depending on the size of the pasta parcels.

3. Pour the cream over the courgettes and add the leaves from the sprigs of sage. Season, bring to the boil and simmer gently for 2–3 minutes, taking care not to boil off too much of the cream.

4. Drain the ravioli and layer on 4 plates with the courgette and cream mixture. Serve at once with the cheese sprinkled over the top.

Pasta Shells with Fresh Beans and Tomato Sauce

❖

MOST pasta dishes need a little Parmesan cheese to set them off, but this one is very good on its own. Start the meal with Spanish Lenten Soup (see page 29) and finish with sliced oranges in fruit juice.

INGREDIENTS

225g (½lb) dried pasta shells
salt
175g (6oz) frozen broad beans
175g (6oz) French beans, topped and
    tailed and cut into 4cm (1½ inch)
    lengths

2 tablespoons olive oil
1 × 400g (14oz) can chopped tomatoes
½ teaspoon sugar
½ teaspoon dried oregano
salt and freshly ground black pepper

◆

1. Cook the pasta shells in boiling salted water for 8–10 minutes or as directed on the pack.

2. Cook the frozen beans in lightly salted boiling water for the length of time given on the pack. Add the French beans about 4 minutes before the end of the cooking time. Drain well.

3. Heat the oil in a deep saucepan and add the chopped tomatoes. Add the sugar, oregano and seasoning and bring to the boil. Cook over a high heat for 4–5 minutes, stirring from time to time. Stir in the beans.

4. Drain the pasta shells and turn into a deep bowl. Pour the bean and tomato mixture over the top. Toss and serve.

CHAPTER NINE

Vegetable Accompaniments

THESE dishes are designed to be served with food from other sections of the book. The recipes concentrate mainly on vegetables which are in season during the winter months although some, such as peas and aubergines, are available all year, either frozen or flown in from other continents.

Some of the dishes freeze well which can be useful. Try making double quantities of the following recipes, keep half for the freezer and use within a month: Curried Lentils, Italian Braised Pumpkin, Gingered Neeps, Baked Rutabaga and Carrot Pudding, and Aubergine-Stuffed Cabbage Leaves.

Shaken Pease

THE name of this recipe is said to come from that of the eighteenth-century pan which was used to cook it – a shaking pan. I think it must have been the equivalent of our frying pan and that is what I use to cook the dish.

This method leaves the sauce quite runny. If you prefer a thicker sauce mix half a teaspoon of cornflour into the sour cream and season accordingly.

INGREDIENTS

25g (1oz) butter
1 onion, peeled and thinly sliced
1 clove garlic, peeled and crushed
350g (12oz) frozen peas
½ cos lettuce, shredded
4 tablespoons sour cream

2 tablespoons white wine or stock
leaves from 4 large sprigs of mint,
   chopped
a pinch of sugar
salt and ground white pepper

---

1. Melt the butter in a small deep-sided frying pan. Add the onion and garlic and cook over a low heat until soft but not brown.

2. Add the peas and shake or stir the pan until they thaw. Continue to cook over a low heat for 2–3 minutes, stirring occasionally.

3. Add all the remaining ingredients and bring to the boil. Simmer for another minute or so and then serve.

VARIATION
◆ Use freshly chopped chervil or parsley in place of mint.

Curried Lentils Ⓥ

❖

THIS developed from a much thicker version of my own recipe for Mulligatawny Soup. It veers more towards the sweet and sour than the red-hot and is based on Southern Indian cuisine rather than Northern Indian or Pakistani cooking.

INGREDIENTS

2 tablespoons cooking oil

1 onion, peeled and sliced

1 clove garlic, peeled and chopped

1 thick stalk of lemon grass

1 tablespoon medium curry powder

75g (3oz) split red lentils

2 leeks, trimmed, cleaned and chopped

1 red pepper, seeded and chopped

1 tablespoon tomato purée

1 tablespoon dark muscovado sugar

salt and freshly ground black pepper

---

1. Heat the oil in a pan and fry the onion, garlic and lemon grass until golden. Add the curry powder and continue to fry for another minute or so.

2. Add all the remaining ingredients, pour in 500ml (16fl oz) water, and bring to the boil. Cover and cook over a low to medium heat for 15–20 minutes. Check the lentils, to see that they are not boiling dry, and stir from time to time.

3. If the mixture is a little too runny thicken by boiling fast, stirring all the time. Remove the lemon grass and serve.

VARIATION

◆ For a much smoother mixture, purée in a blender or rub through a sieve. Reheat and serve garnished with the juice of 1 lemon and 2 tablespoons freshly chopped chives.

Beetroot with Apples

❖

THERE is a really interesting blend of flavours in this dish from Central Russia. The sweetness of the beetroot balances the sourness of the cooking apple and the two are offset by the ginger. Serve with Brussels Sprouts with Nutmeg Breadcrumbs (see page 115) and Grated Potato Cakes (see page 94).

INGREDIENTS

450g (1lb) raw beetroot, peeled and grated
200ml (8fl oz) vegetable stock
1 large cooking apple, peeled, cored and grated

1 teaspoon freshly grated root ginger
salt and freshly ground black pepper
1 tablespoon cider vinegar or white wine vinegar

◆

1. Place the beetroot in a saucepan with the stock and bring to the boil. Cover and cook over a low heat for about 15 minutes.

2. Add the apple, ginger and seasoning and cook for another 5 minutes. Add the vinegar and turn up the heat to boil off the excess liquid. Stir frequently to avoid burning.

VARIATIONS

◆ This dish is often cooked with 3–4 tablespoons sour cream. The result is much richer and is delicious served with plain grilled vegetables.

◆ Alternatively you can cook the beetroot with the juice of 1 orange, a little grated orange rind and a knob of butter. Omit the vinegar and ginger.

Hanseatic Kohlrabi and Carrots

❖

KOHLRABI is much more popular in Germany than it is in the UK, but supplies are gradually starting to appear in British shops. It actually grows on the stems of the plants rather like a solid sprout. The flavour is slightly reminiscent of sprouts too.

Peel the kohlrabi as thinly as you can and then grate coarsely for quick cooking.

INGREDIENTS

225g (½lb) kohlrabi, peeled and coarsely grated
225g (½lb) carrots, peeled and coarsely grated
300ml (½ pint) milk or soya milk

2 tablespoons cooking oil
15g (½oz) plain flour
1 tablespoon freshly chopped dill
salt and freshly ground black pepper

◆

1. Place the vegetables in a pan and cover with the milk or soya milk. Bring to the boil and reduce the heat. Cover and simmer for 20 minutes until soft.

2. Heat the oil in another pan and add the flour. Stir over a medium heat until the mixture bubbles.

3. Using the tip of a teaspoon add small amounts of the oil and flour mixture to the cooked vegetables, stirring all the time. Add the dill and seasoning and bring to the boil.

4. Continue to boil gently for 2–3 minutes to ensure that the flour is cooked through. Serve at once.

Brussels Sprouts with Nutmeg Breadcrumbs

❖

THIS recipe for crunchy coated Brussels sprouts amalgamates ideas from Holland and Hungary. The nutmeg is the Dutch contribution – I have often been served steamed sprouts sprinkled with nutmeg in Holland. The breadcrumb coating for sprouts comes from a restaurant in Central Hungary which I visited on a wine-tasting tour of the country.

The flavour is very much better if made with butter, but a good cooking oil can be used in its place.

INGREDIENTS

450g (1lb) Brussels sprouts, trimmed and
   cleaned
salt
75g (3oz) butter or 4 tablespoons
   cooking oil

115g (4oz) fresh breadcrumbs
½ teaspoon ground nutmeg
salt and freshly ground black pepper

◆

---

1. Cook the sprouts in a little salted water for about 15 minutes until just tender and drain thoroughly.

2. Meanwhile heat the butter or oil in a frying pan and add the breadcrumbs. Fry over a medium heat until well browned. Mix in the nutmeg and seasoning.

3. Add the drained sprouts to the pan and turn them over several times until they are well coated with crispy breadcrumbs. Serve at once.

VARIATION
◆ Fry some finely chopped nuts with the breadcrumbs. Try pecan nuts, walnuts or peanuts.

Gingered Neeps

I N SCOTLAND the word neeps usually refers to large yellow or pink swedes, not to small white turnips, and swede is the best vegetable to use in this unusual recipe. Don't stint on the butter – it really is essential for the very best results.

INGREDIENTS

450g (1lb) swede, peeled and diced
salt
25g (1oz) butter
2 cloves

½ bunch spring onions, trimmed and
   finely chopped
1 tablespoon freshly grated root ginger
ground white pepper

1. Cook the swede in a steamer, or in very little salted boiling water, for 15–20 minutes until just tender.

2. Melt the butter in a pan and fry the cloves for about 30 seconds over a low heat. Then add the spring onions and ginger and continue frying for 3–4 minutes.

3. Mash the cooked swede and add it to the onion and ginger. Season, stir well together and serve at once.

VARIATION

◆ If you really do not want to use butter, try 2 tablespoons well-flavoured olive oil instead.

Aubergine-Stuffed Cabbage Leaves Ⓥ

❖

T HE best leaves to use for this recipe are large ones from bunches of spring greens. Keep the smaller leaves to steam and serve as a side dish.

───────── INGREDIENTS ─────────

8 large cabbage leaves

1 onion, peeled and finely chopped

1 clove garlic, peeled and crushed

2 tablespoons olive oil

1 medium aubergine

2 tablespoons unhulled sesame seeds

150ml (¼ pint) tomato juice

juice of 1 lemon

a few sprigs of fresh mint

salt and freshly ground black pepper

150g (5oz) tofu, finely diced

1. Place the cabbage leaves in a deep dish or tin and pour boiling water over them to soften the stalks. Leave to stand in the water until needed.

2. Fry the onion and garlic in the olive oil for 2–3 minutes to soften a little. Do not allow them to brown.

3. Peel the aubergine and dice very finely indeed. Add to the pan and stir. Add the sesame seeds, 3 tablespoons of the tomato juice, the lemon juice, mint and seasoning. Stir over a medium heat for 4–5 minutes.

4. Transfer the contents of the pan to a bowl and stir in the tofu, mashing the mixture lightly with a fork.

5. Drain the cabbage leaves and dry them on kitchen paper. Spoon a little of the aubergine mixture into the centre of each leaf and roll up into a parcel.

6. Place the parcels in a saucepan and pour on the rest of the tomato juice. Bring to the boil, reduce the heat and cover. Simmer in the tomato juice for 10 minutes before serving.

Baked Rutabaga and Carrot Pudding

RUTABAGA is the name Americans give the humble swede. I have deliberately used this transatlantic name in the title to encourage you to look at the recipe and not turn over simply because it uses swede!

This dish is both colourful and tasty and it makes an excellent main course with a couple of other vegetable dishes such as Broccoli Hotpot (see page 76) and Indian Mashed Potato (see page 95).

INGREDIENTS

500g (1lb 2oz) rutabaga or swede, peeled and very finely chopped or coarsely grated
boiling vegetable stock
500g (1lb 2oz) carrots, peeled and very finely chopped or coarsely grated

115ml (4fl oz) double cream
3 tablespoons freshly chopped chives
2–3 large sprigs of fresh tarragon, chopped
salt and freshly ground black pepper

1. Place the swede in a small saucepan and just cover with boiling vegetable stock. Return to the boil and cook for 8–10 minutes until just tender.

2. Place the carrot in another small saucepan and just cover with boiling vegetable stock. Return to the boil and cook for 6–7 minutes until tender.

3. Drain the vegetables very well, retaining the stock for use in soup. Mash the swede with a fork and stir in half the cream and all the chives. Then mash the carrots and add the rest of the cream and the tarragon. Season both vegetable mixtures.

4. Spoon the carrot into the base of a small pudding basin and press well down. Top with the swede and press well down again.

5. Cover the basin with clingfilm and place in a saucepan with about 2.5cm (1 inch) hot water in the base. Bring to the boil and simmer for 10 minutes or until required.

Italian Braised Pumpkin

❖

PUMPKIN is often considered an American speciality but the Italians also use pumpkin in some casseroles and in their pasta parcels. This recipe produces a wonderfully garlicky mixture which can be served as a side dish or used to stuff other vegetables such as blanched spinach leaves or grilled mushrooms.

INGREDIENTS

25g (1oz) butter or soya margarine
200ml (8fl oz) dry white wine or half and half wine and vegetable stock
2 large cloves garlic, peeled and coarsely chopped

450g (1lb) peeled and chopped pumpkin
salt and freshly ground black pepper
2–3 tablespoons freshly chopped parsley

◆

1. Heat the butter or margarine and wine in a saucepan and add the garlic.

2. Dice the pumpkin fairly small to ensure that it cooks through in the time. Add to the pan, season, and return to the boil.

3. Reduce the heat and cover. Cook for about 20 minutes over a medium heat, stirring from time to time. Do not allow the liquid to dry out completely until the pumpkin is cooked. Then, if there is some liquid left, boil it off quickly.

4. Stir in the parsley and serve.

Hungarian Cabbage Pancake

WHITE cabbage would probably be the local choice for this dish from the Upper Danube, but I tried it with a firm green cabbage and the results were very good indeed. This size cabbage pancake will serve four people as a side dish to accompany a casserole from Chapter 6.

Alternatively it would make a satisfying main dish for two hungry people, served with a bowl of stewed apples and some thick spiced yogurt.

—————————— INGREDIENTS ——————————

400g (14oz) cabbage, trimmed and very
   finely shredded
1 whole clove garlic, peeled
2 eggs

4 tablespoons fresh breadcrumbs
½ teaspoon dried sage
salt and ground white pepper
1 tablespoon cooking oil

1. Place the shredded cabbage in a saucepan with the garlic. Cover with water and bring to the boil. Cook over a medium heat for about 10 minutes until the cabbage is tender. If you have a little more time, cook the cabbage and garlic in a steamer.

2. Drain the cooked cabbage and dry on kitchen paper. Discard the garlic. Beat the eggs with the breadcrumbs, sage and seasoning and stir into the cabbage.

3. Heat the oil in an 18cm (7 inch) frying pan and add the cabbage and egg mixture. Spread out like a large thick pancake. Fry for 3–4 minutes until browned on the base. Finish off under a hot grill. Serve cut into wedges.

VARIATION

♦ Use 1 dessertspoon freshly chopped dill or a pinch of caraway seeds in place of the sage.

Celeriac with Yogurt and Potatoes

I LIKE this dish because you can throw all the vegetables in together and leave them to cook into a wonderfully flavourful mass. I sometimes stir in some fresh herbs just before serving but it is very good without.

Serve with dry dishes such as filo pies, fritters, vegeburgers or grilled cheese.

INGREDIENTS

1 onion, peeled and sliced
1 tablespoon cooking oil
450g (1lb) celeriac, peeled and finely diced
200g (7oz) carrots, peeled and finely diced

350g (12oz) potatoes, peeled and diced
½ green pepper, seeded and chopped
4 tablespoons yogurt
2 tablespoons vegetable stock
salt and freshly ground black pepper

1. Gently fry the onion in the oil for 1–2 minutes and then add the celeriac and carrots. Continue to cook gently for 3–4 minutes, stirring from time to time.

2. Add all the remaining ingredients and bring to the boil. Reduce the heat and cover. Simmer for about 15 minutes, stirring regularly to stop the mixture burning.

3. Check to see if the vegetables are all cooked through, and continue cooking for another 5 minutes if necessary. This will probably depend upon how finely you have diced the vegetables.

VARIATIONS

◆ Use 3 tablespoons frozen peas or broad beans in place of the green pepper.

◆ Stir in some freshly chopped herbs just before serving.

Spicy Broccoli with Water Chestnuts

THIS recipe is inspired by the spicy cooking of Sichuan China and I have had Chinese and Eastern greens cooked in this manner – you might even try it with cabbage. However I particularly like the crunchy spicy effect with broccoli which can so easily become soggy with other methods of cooking.

It is very good served with Six Jewel Rice (see page 89).

INGREDIENTS

350–400g (12–14oz) head broccoli
3 tablespoons cooking oil
3 cloves garlic, peeled and thinly sliced
2.5cm (1 inch) fresh root ginger, peeled and thinly sliced
1 × 225g (8oz) can water chestnuts, drained

2 tablespoons soy sauce with chilli or
1 tablespoon plain soy sauce and
1 tablespoon with chilli
1 tablespoon roasted sesame oil
a pinch of five spice powder

1. Cut the stems of the broccoli into short lengths on the slant. Break the heads into smaller pieces if very large.

2. Heat the oil in a wok or deep frying pan and fry the garlic and ginger for 30 seconds. Add the broccoli and continue stir-frying for 2 minutes.

3. Add the water chestnuts, soy sauce, sesame oil and five spice powder and toss all the ingredients well together, making sure the broccoli is well coated in the sauce.

4. Cover and cook over a medium heat for another 1–2 minutes until the broccoli is as crisp or as tender as you like it and the sauce has reduced a little.

CHAPTER TEN

Winter Salads

SALAD does not have to consist only of lettuce, tomato and cucumber. Anyway, these vegetables are not in particularly good supply during the winter months and those which are on sale do not always have a very good flavour.

There are, however, many other vegetables which can be used in salads during the winter. All the root vegetables are excellent freshly grated. Simply toss in a little salad or olive oil to prevent them discolouring and drying up. Add shredded cabbage, kale, sprouts, spinach, cauliflower and broccoli, leeks and kohlrabi to the list and you have a really wide choice.

The salads in this section are designed to be eaten as side dishes with a main course but they can also be used in a salad medley to make up a meal in their own right. Try Green Cabbage Salad with Fruit and Nut Salad and Leek and Horseradish Salad or Mixed Winter Vegetable Salad with Fennel, Chicory and Apple Salad and Kohlrabi and Red Pepper Salad.

Some of them can also be served as first courses. Taco Salad and Tabouleh with chicory spears work well like this.

Green Cabbage Salad Ⓥ

❖

GREEN cabbage leaves of various kinds are available throughout the winter months and there is no reason why they should always be cooked. Indeed they work very well in salads. The only point to watch is that the outer leaves can be a little tough and will need to be shredded even more finely than the others.

This salad is designed to accompany dishes such as Ravioli with Sage and Courgettes (see page 108) or Polenta Pie (see page 70). It can also be served in a medley of different salads.

—————————— INGREDIENTS ——————————

½ green cabbage or 2 heads spring
   greens
1 carrot, peeled and grated
3 tablespoons raisins

DRESSING
3 tablespoons salad oil
1 tablespoon fresh orange juice
1 teaspoon lemon juice
a little grated orange rind
freshly ground black pepper

◆

1. Cut out the thick stalks and shred the cabbage as finely as you can. Place in a bowl and mix with the grated carrot and raisins.

2. Mix all the dressing ingredients together and pour over the salad. Toss and serve.

Mixed Winter Vegetable Salad

❖

THIS salad includes cabbage and also makes use of the most common seasonal vegetables. You can substitute whatever you happen to have in the vegetable rack for one or other of the vegetables given here.

INGREDIENTS

1 large carrot, peeled and coarsely grated

1 parsnip, peeled and coarsely grated

juice of 1 lemon

¼ cabbage (Savoy, red, green or white), very finely shredded

1 small onion, peeled and cut into fine rings

2 medium-sized cooked beetroot, diced

3 tablespoons salad oil

salt and freshly ground black pepper

---

1. Place the grated carrot and parsnip in a large bowl. Add the lemon juice and toss well to avoid any discolouration.

2. Add the remaining vegetables, the oil and seasoning and toss well. The salad can now be kept in the fridge for up to half an hour before serving.

VARIATION

◆ This salad becomes quite exotic with the addition of 1 tablespoon light soy sauce. Mix with the oil and add at the end.

Fennel and Honey Slaw

THIS well-flavoured slaw makes a change from the usual cabbage and carrot mixture on sale in the supermarket. The idea comes from a Canadian friend who really fell for the taste of fennel on a recent visit to Italy. The other ingredients are from her regular coleslaw recipe.

There is no need to blanch the vegetables if you like a very crunchy slaw.

—— INGREDIENTS ——

175g (6oz) white cabbage, very finely
  shredded
1 large head fennel, cut in half and very
  finely shredded
2 sticks celery, cut into thin sticks 4cm
  (1½ inches) in length
150ml (¼ pint) sour cream or thick
  yogurt

1 tablespoon runny honey
1 tablespoon vinegar
½ teaspoon made mustard
¼ teaspoon cayenne pepper
a little salt

1. Mix the cabbage, fennel and celery in a bowl and cover with boiling water. Leave to stand for 1 minute and drain. Then plunge the vegetables into very cold water. Drain again and dry on kitchen paper. Return to the dry bowl.

2. Mix all the remaining ingredients together and pour over the vegetables. Toss well so that everything is covered with the dressing. Serve at once.

Fennel, Chicory and Apple Salad

❖

ALL THESE ingredients are fairly easy to find during the winter months and together they make an unusual salad.

Serve this as a crunchy first course before a casserole or curry from Chapter 6 or with Mixed Winter Vegetable Salad (see page 125) and Kohlrabi and Red Pepper Salad (see page 133).

―――――― INGREDIENTS ――――――

1 medium-sized head fennel, trimmed
juice of ½ lemon
2 green apples, cored and diced

2 heads chicory, sliced
2 tablespoons extra virgin olive oil
salt and freshly ground black pepper

◆

1. Shred the fennel as finely as you can and mix with the lemon juice. Place in the fridge for 15 minutes or until required.

2. Add the apple and chicory and mix well. Pour on the olive oil and season to taste. Toss well and serve.

VARIATIONS

◆ For a creamier salad use mayonnaise in place of olive oil.

◆ Add chopped smoked tofu, hard-boiled eggs or cubes of cheese to make a more substantial dish.

Leek and Horseradish Salad

Tʜɪs Western version of Indian raita makes a refreshing side dish to serve with the curries in Chapter 6.

Small, thin or even baby leeks are the best choice for this recipe. Cut them into short lengths before steaming. You can use larger, older leeks if you wish but they will need to be sliced quite thinly.

It is important to catch the leeks while they still retain some bite and before they are fully cooked. I usually try to test a small piece every minute or so. Plunge them under cold water as soon as you think they are ready. This will cool them and prevent further cooking.

INGREDIENTS

450g (1lb) leeks, trimmed, cleaned and sliced as described above

DRESSING
4–6 spring onions, trimmed and finely chopped

4 tablespoons thick yogurt
1 tablespoon cider vinegar
2 tablespoons freshly chopped parsley
1 teaspoon grated horseradish
salt and freshly ground black pepper

1. Place the leeks in a steamer over boiling water. Cover and cook for 6–8 minutes depending on size.

2. Mix all the dressing ingredients together and leave to stand until required.

3. Drain the leeks and dry them on kitchen paper. Toss with the prepared dressing and serve at once.

VARIATION
♦ Serve with sliced goat's cheese and tomatoes to make a more substantial dish to use as a first course or supper dish.

Taco Salad

❖

THIS crunchy salad has a very definite Mexican theme and you can add or subtract ingredients as you wish. Restrict your choice to salad leaves, avocado and tacos and you have an excellent side salad to serve with a main course dish. Alternatively you can add beans, olives and cheese to make an all-in-one meal.

INGREDIENTS

1 small avocado, peeled, stoned and cubed
1 tablespoon lemon juice
mixed salad leaves
½ bunch or bag of watercress
5–6 sprigs of fresh coriander
3–4 sun-dried peppers or 5–6 sun-dried tomatoes, shredded

1 green chilli, seeded and cut into very thin rings (optional)
75g (3oz) plain tacos or tortilla chips, coarsely crushed

DRESSING
3 tablespoons olive oil
2 teaspoons wine or cider vinegar
salt and freshly ground black pepper

1. Prepare the avocado and mix with the lemon juice at once to avoid any discolouration.

2. Mix the salad leaves with the watercress and coriander in a large bowl.

3. Add the avocado, sun-dried peppers or tomatoes, chilli if using, and crushed tacos or tortilla chips.

4. Mix all the dressing ingredients together and pour over the salad. Toss well and serve at once. (If you leave the salad to stand the tortilla chips will go soggy.)

VARIATION
◆ Add 4 tablespoons cooked or canned red kidney beans, 8–12 stoned black olives and 100g (3½oz) cubed Cheddar cheese.

Beetroot and Orange Salad
with Horseradish

❖

FRESH horseradish needs a very sharp knife to peel it and the juice can sting your eyes, so wear thin rubber or plastic gloves and keep your fingers away from your eyes. I find that it is much easier to look out for jars of ready-grated horseradish which can be stored in the fridge for quite a long time.

Remember that both the freshly grated root and the ready-grated horseradish are much stronger than creamed horseradish. If you use the latter you will need to add 1 tablespoon more than the quantity given in the recipe.

—————————— INGREDIENTS ——————————

225g (½lb) raw beetroot, peeled
3 spring onions, finely chopped
2 tablespoons olive oil
1 green eating apple

1 tablespoon lemon juice
1 orange
½–1 teaspoon grated horseradish
salt and freshly ground black pepper

◆

1. Finely grate the beetroot into a bowl. This is best done in an electric food processor if you have one. Stir in the spring onion and olive oil.

2. Core and dice the apple and immediately mix with the lemon juice to avoid any discolouration.

3. Grate a little of the orange zest into the beetroot mixture and stir in the grated horseradish and seasoning.

4. Peel the orange and remove all the pith. Break into segments and cut each segment into 4–5 small pieces. Add to the beetroot mixture. Stir and serve when required.

Fruit and Nut Salad ⓥ

❖

THIS is a really chunky salad which can be served on its own or as part of a medley of salads. If you are planning to make it the main part of the meal you should increase the quantities by about a third.

─────────── INGREDIENTS ───────────

some soft lettuce leaves
2 green apples
2 bananas
juice of ½ lemon
2 tablespoons raisins
½ head celery, trimmed and chopped
1 small red pepper, seeded and chopped
50g (2oz) cashew nuts

50g (2oz) pistachio nuts
25g (1oz) sunflower seeds
a few whole chives

DRESSING
3 tablespoons salad oil
a little cider vinegar
freshly ground black pepper

1. Arrange the lettuce leaves on 4 plates.

2. Core and dice the apples, and peel and slice the bananas. Toss in the lemon juice as soon as they are cut to avoid discolouration. Stir in the raisins, celery and red pepper.

3. Dry-fry the nuts and sunflower seeds in a frying pan over a medium heat. Keep stirring the nuts to stop them burning. When they are lightly browned add them to the salad and spoon the mixture over the lettuce leaves.

4. Mix the dressing ingredients together and pour over the salads. Garnish each portion with long sprigs of chive.

Tabouleh

❖

THERE are numerous different recipes for this popular Middle Eastern salad, but they all rely heavily on freshly chopped flat-leaf parsley. This is a fairly elaborate version which I like to make when I am going to serve the salad as part of a salad medley. It has lots of colour and flavour. It can also be used to stuff chicory spears, cherry tomato halves and celery sticks.

—————————— INGREDIENTS ——————————

75g (3oz) bulgur or cracked wheat
1 large bunch of flat-leaf parsley, finely chopped
4 spring onions, trimmed and finely chopped
2 tomatoes, skinned, seeded and chopped
7.5cm (3 inches) cucumber, diced

½ green pepper, seeded and finely chopped
3 tablespoons finely chopped mint
1 tablespoon paprika
juice of 1 lemon
3 tablespoons olive oil
salt and freshly ground black pepper

◆

1. Place the bulgur wheat in a bowl and cover with cold water. Leave to stand for 20 minutes.

2. Prepare all the remaining ingredients while the bulgur is soaking. Mix together in a bowl.

3. Drain the bulgur well and then squeeze out all the water with your hands. Dry on kitchen paper. Stir into the other ingredients.

4. Taste to check the seasoning and add a little more lemon juice if you like a sharper flavour.

VARIATIONS

◆ Use 100g (3½oz) no-soak dried apricots, finely chopped, and 25g (1oz) toasted pinenuts in place of the tomatoes and cucumber.

◆ For a really simple salad use only the bulgur, parsley, spring onion, mint, lemon juice and olive oil.

Kohlrabi and Red Pepper Salad

❖

Raw kohlrabi has a lovely crunchy texture which stands up well to this warm Oriental-style dressing.

Serve with Fennel and Honey Slaw (see page 126) and a green salad or on its own as a first course.

INGREDIENTS

1 large kohlrabi, peeled
1 large red pepper, seeded and shredded
2 sticks celery, trimmed and finely sliced
3 tablespoons roasted peanuts
1 tablespoon freshly chopped mint leaves

WARM DRESSING
4 tablespoons salad oil
2 tablespoons light soy sauce
2 teaspoons cider vinegar
salt and freshly ground black pepper

◆

1. Finely slice the kohlrabi and then cut into thin sticks. Place in a bowl and mix with the pepper, celery, peanuts and mint.

2. Mix all the dressing ingredients together in a small saucepan and heat gently. Do not allow the mixture to get too hot. Pour over the salad and serve at once.

VARIATIONS

◆ Use coriander instead of mint and add a pinch of five spice powder. Take care not to use too much or it will dominate the other flavours.

◆ Use mooli or Jerusalem artichoke instead of kohlrabi.

Italian Cheese and Walnut Salad

THIS salad comes from the hill villages of Tuscany where it is served as a mid-morning snack, as part of a cold buffet of local produce or as a quick starter for the main meal of the day. In Italy the cheese is always Pecorino ewe's milk cheese, but you can use any hard ewe's milk cheese. Use the best-quality olive oil you have, as this is an important part of the flavouring.

Be sure to include some rocket or watercress in the mixture of salad leaves. The piquant taste greatly adds to the flavour of the salad. Some of the more unusual winter salad leaves on sale in organic and specialist shops have a similar effect.

INGREDIENTS

½ small ciabatta loaf or well-flavoured white bread
1–2 cloves garlic
mixed salad leaves
175g (6oz) Pecorino or hard vegetarian ewe's milk cheese, diced

4 tablespoons walnut halves, coarsely chopped
a small bunch of parsley, freshly chopped
well-flavoured extra virgin olive oil
a little lemon juice (optional)

1. Cut the bread into thick slices and rub each side with a cut clove of garlic, retaining any garlic left. Toast the bread until it is lightly seared. Leave to cool.

2. Dice the bread and toss with the salad leaves, cheese, walnuts and parsley. Spoon onto 4 plates.

3. Pour plenty of olive oil over each salad. The quantity is up to you, but use at least 1 tablespoon per person.

4. If you like, you can sprinkle a little lemon juice over each salad but this is not really necessary and is not authentically Italian.

— CHAPTER ELEVEN —

Snacks

THIS chapter looks at ideas for quick snacks which you can quickly prepare as you dash in and out to other activities.

Some of the recipes, such as Garlic and Tomato Salsa Toasts, Curried Banana Toasts and Spicy Cheese Boats, can be cut into smaller portions and used as party food.

As usual in this book my inspiration has come from around the world and there are crostini from Italy, mushroom dishes from Austria, quesadillas and tacos from Mexico and Feta cheese dishes from Greece.

Garlic and Tomato Salsa Toasts

❖

THIS recipe is guaranteed to give even unripe winter tomatoes a touch of Mexican sunshine! Serve at any time on lengths of French bread.

—— INGREDIENTS ——

4 × 23cm (9 inch) small French loaves
1 whole clove garlic, peeled
4 tablespoons olive oil
6–8 tomatoes, seeded and diced
1 small bunch of spring onions, trimmed
    and chopped

1 green chilli, seeded and chopped
6 tablespoons freshly chopped coriander
juice of ½ lemon
freshly ground black pepper

1. Cut the loaves in half lengthways. Rub all over with the clove of garlic and brush with some of the olive oil. Place under a hot grill and cook on both sides until lightly browned.

2. Meanwhile, mix all the remaining ingredients in a bowl. Spread the mixture over the cut side of each piece of French bread and return to the grill. Cook for a further 2–3 minutes. Drizzle with the remaining olive oil and serve at once.

VARIATION

◆ Use lime juice in place of the lemon juice and add a little freshly grated root ginger to the mixture.

Curried Banana Toasts

❖

THIS banana mixture can be used cold to make open or closed sandwiches but when it is grilled it seems to take on a new dimension. The mixture also works very successfully in a toasted sandwich maker.

You can use a block of dried dates or the kind of dates that come in boxes at Christmas. The latter are easier to mash but they need to be stoned. You will also need to use rather more of them to allow for the weight of the stones.

INGREDIENTS

4 large chunky slices of wholemeal bread
4 large bananas, peeled
a little grated lemon rind
2 tablespoons mango chutney

175g (6oz) dried dates, chopped and mashed
1 teaspoon curry powder
salt and freshly ground black pepper

1. Toast the bread well on the first side and lightly on the second side.

2. Mash the bananas and immediately mix with the lemon rind and chutney. Then mix in the rest of the ingredients to make a thick paste.

3. Spread this mixture on the lightly toasted side of the bread and return to the grill. Cook for about 5 minutes, until the mixture bubbles, and serve at once.

VARIATION

◆ Sprinkle grated cheese over the top of the banana mixture when it has been under the grill for about 3 minutes. (Allow about 115g (4oz) for 4 slices of toast.) Toasted sandwiches are also very good with cheese added to the curried banana mixture.

Avocado and Pinenut Crostini Ⓥ

❖

THIS quantity will serve four people as a snack. There are a number of roast nut oils on the market now. I used the French Cacahuetes Grillé, but roasted sesame oil would work just as well.

―――――――――― INGREDIENTS ――――――――――

1 ciabatta loaf
1 whole clove garlic, peeled
2 large avocados, peeled and stoned
juice of ½ lemon
50g (2oz) toasted pinenuts, roughly
  chopped

4 tablespoons freshly chopped basil
salt and freshly ground black pepper
3 large beefsteak tomatoes, thickly sliced
2 tablespoons roasted nut oil

1. Slice the ciabatta loaf in half lengthways through the centre and open out. Cut each large flat slice in half.

2. Toast the ciabatta on each side and rub with the clove of garlic.

3. Dice the avocados and mix with the lemon juice to avoid any discolouration. Carefully mix in the toasted pinenuts, basil and seasoning.

4. Arrange the tomato slices on the toasted ciabatta, season and grill for a further 2–3 minutes. Top with the avocado mixture, drizzle with roasted nut oil and serve at once.

VARIATION
◆ Use freshly chopped coriander instead of basil for a punchier flavour.

Greek Cheese and Olives on Toast

I USUALLY use a very mild Swiss or German mustard for this recipe but if you like strong mustard you may prefer to use Dijon or English. Remember that Feta cheese hardens rather than melts under the heat so take care not to over-cook it.

INGREDIENTS

4 large slices dark rye or rye and whole-meal bread

4 tablespoons made mustard

12 large Greek olives, stoned and coarsely chopped

175g (6oz) Feta cheese with olive oil and oregano, crumbled

extra virgin olive oil

some freshly chopped chives and parsley

1. Toast the bread properly on one side and lightly on the second side. Spread the second side with the mustard and top with the olives and cheese.

2. Return to the grill and cook for 2–3 minutes. Drizzle with olive oil and garnish with fresh chives and parsley.

VARIATION

◆ Add some sliced tomatoes for a moister topping.

Mushroom and Cheese Sauté

THE inspiration for this rich, warming snack comes from the Austrian Alps where wild mushrooms abound. The quantities are sufficient for two generous servings on large rounds of toast. Simply double up if you want to make enough for four.

INGREDIENTS

15g (½oz) dried wild mushrooms
25g (1oz) butter
1 tablespoon oil
200g (7oz) button mushrooms, thinly
   sliced
1 tablespoon brandy

2 large slices of bread
3 tablespoons grated Bergkäse or
   Emmental cheese
a pinch of nutmeg
salt and freshly ground black pepper
2 large sprigs of flat-leaf parsley

1. Place the wild mushrooms in a mug and barely cover with boiling water. Leave to stand for 15 minutes.

2. Heat the butter and oil in a small frying pan and add the fresh mushrooms. Sauté gently over a low heat for 5 minutes.

3. Add the wild mushrooms and their liquid and bring to the boil. Add the brandy and cook over a high heat for 3–4 minutes until all the liquid evaporates.

4. Toast the bread until lightly seared.

5. Add 2 tablespoons grated cheese, the nutmeg and seasoning to the mushroom mixture. Pile onto the prepared toast. Sprinkle with the remaining cheese and decorate each portion with a large sprig of flat-leaf parsley.

Spicy Cheese Boats

WHEN they are lined up on the serving dish these French bread snacks look just like a narrowboat marina – hence the name! They make a filling snack at any time of day.

I used Emmental cheese to test the recipe but if you want to be sure of vegetarian rennet you can use vegetarian Cheddar instead. Make sure you buy mature cheese to give a good robust flavour.

INGREDIENTS

150ml (¼ pint) mayonnaise
150g (5oz) finely grated Emmental or vegetarian Cheddar cheese
8–10 spring onions, trimmed and finely chopped
2 tablespoons freshly chopped basil

1 tablespoon soy sauce with chilli or ordinary soy sauce with a few drops of Tabasco sauce
plenty of freshly ground black pepper
4 x 23cm (9 inch) small French loaves
a few sprigs of fresh basil

1. Set the oven to 180°C/350°F/Gas Mark 4.

2. Mix the mayonnaise in a bowl with the cheese, spring onions, basil, soy sauce and black pepper.

3. Cut the loaves in half lengthways and spread each cut side with the cheese mixture.

4. Place on a baking tray and bake for 10–15 minutes until lightly browned on top. Serve garnished with sprigs of fresh basil.

VARIATION

◆ Slice 2 tomatoes and arrange on top of the bread before spreading on the cheese mixture. Alternatively use 1 tomato and serve everyone with a plain slice and a tomato slice.

Buddhist Eggs

THESE eggs are cooked using a steam-fry combination method which keeps the fat content to a minimum and allows you to flavour the eggs at the same time.

Serve them on thick hunks of dense bread which will soak up all the juices. Or you can accompany them with reheated left-over cereals such as couscous, bulgur or polenta. If you have more time, Buddhist eggs are very good on jacket potatoes.

INGREDIENTS
---

2 teaspoons cooking oil

4 eggs

4–6 tablespoons vegetable stock, tomato or carrot juice

salt and freshly ground black pepper

TOPPINGS

4 tablespoons finely grated hard cheese

4 tablespoons finely chopped green and red peppers

2 tablespoons finely chopped sun-dried tomatoes

---

1. Heat the oil in a small frying pan with a lid. Break the eggs into the pan and cook for 15–20 seconds until the bases set. (If you use eggs straight from the fridge this will take a little longer.)

2. Pour the stock or juice round the eggs and season. Then cover the eggs with your chosen topping. If you use toppings together adjust the quantities accordingly.

3. Cover and leave to cook for 1–2 minutes, depending on how well done you like your eggs. Serve at once.

Sesame Stuffed Mushrooms

❖

USE large flat field mushrooms for this excellent snack and double the quantities if everyone is hungry. Serve with warm rolls.

INGREDIENTS

4 large flat field mushrooms
6 tablespoons olive oil
3 tablespoons tahini
1 clove garlic, peeled and crushed

2 tablespoons freshly chopped parsley
1 teaspoon ready-made mint sauce
salt and freshly ground black pepper
1–2 teaspoons sesame seeds

1. Cut the stalks out of the field mushrooms and keep on one side. Brush the caps with some of the olive oil and place under a hot grill for about 5 minutes. Turn over, brush the gills with the remaining oil and grill for a further 5 minutes. Test with a fork to see if the mushrooms are fully cooked or if they need another 1–2 minutes.

2. Meanwhile chop the retained mushroom stalks very finely and mix with the tahini, garlic, parsley, mint sauce and seasoning. Add a little water to make the mixture spreadable.

3. When the mushrooms are cooked spread them with the tahini mixture and sprinkle with the sesame seeds. Place under a hot grill and cook for about 5 minutes until well browned. Serve at once.

Quesadillas

IF YOU do not want to be bothered with all the spicing ingredients you can buy a small jar of Mexican spices in oil and use it for this and other Mexican dishes. If you like really hot food add some sliced jalapeño chillies.

These quesadillas are quite filling but if you are very hungry you could well eat two. There are usually eight tortillas in a pack so all you need to do is double the quantities of the sauce, cheese and coriander.

INGREDIENTS

4 flour tortillas
2 tablespoons olive oil
175g (6oz) smoked cheese, grated
4 large sprigs of fresh coriander

SAUCE
1 × 400g (14oz) can chopped tomatoes
2 cloves garlic, peeled and crushed

1 green or red chilli, seeded and
 chopped
1 teaspoon paprika
½ teaspoon ground cumin
½ teaspoon dried oregano
salt and freshly ground black pepper

1. Start by making the sauce. Empty the contents of the can of tomatoes into a small saucepan and add the garlic, chilli, paprika, cumin, oregano and seasoning. Bring to the boil and cook over a medium heat for 6–8 minutes to thicken the mixture.

2. Brush the tortillas on both sides with the oil and stack in a frying pan with a lid. Cover and cook over a medium heat to soften them. Turn to warm through but do not allow them to crisp.

3. Spread each tortilla with the sauce and sprinkle on the cheese. Top with a sprig of coriander. Fold over and replace in the frying pan.

4. Cook over a medium heat for 2–3 minutes until golden. Turn over and cook the other side. Serve at once.

Taco Shells with Cauliflower and Guacamole Filling

❖

M ANY shops now sell ready-made guacamole, and pickled beetroot is no problem, so this is a very quick snack to make. If you like very spicy food you can pep up the guacamole by adding some chilli.

---------------------------------- INGREDIENTS ----------------------------------

1 packet of 12 taco shells
550g (1¼lb) cauliflower
2 tablespoons olive oil
½ contents of a 350g (12oz) jar pickled
   beetroot, drained

shredded lettuce
2 × 115g (4oz) cartons of guacamole

---

1. Heat the oven as directed on the pack of taco shells and follow the instructions for heating them through.

2. Cut the cauliflower into florets so that it will cook quickly and place in a steamer over a pan of boiling water. Cover and cook for 6–8 minutes, depending on the size of the florets. They should still have a bit of bite to them.

3. Cut the cauliflower into smaller pieces and toss with the oil. Chop the beetroot.

4. Remove the taco shells from the oven and fill each one with a little shredded lettuce. Then add the dressed cauliflower. Top with a spoonful of guacamole and some pickled beetroot. Serve at once.

VARIATIONS

◆ Use hummus instead of guacamole and mix with freshly chopped coriander.

◆ Top with chopped capers mixed with toasted pinenuts instead of pickled beetroot.

Drop Scones with Smoked Tofu and Shredded Vegetables

❖

THIS is another East/West improvisation which uses a childhood favourite of mine – Scottish drop scones – as a base for a Japanese-style topping. If you do not have time to prepare the vegetables for the topping, try serving Japanese sliced and preserved ginger with the tofu instead.

─── INGREDIENTS ───

225g (8oz) wholemeal self-raising flour
½ teaspoon cream of tartar
¼ teaspoon salt
2 eggs, beaten
300ml (½ pint) soya milk
1 teaspoon freshly grated root ginger
4 spring onions, finely chopped
115g (4oz) sweetcorn kernels

TOPPINGS
1 large carrot, peeled and coarsely grated
¼ segment of a small white cabbage, finely shredded
1 piece of lemon grass
1 tablespoon heavy soy sauce
250g (9oz) block smoked tofu, cut into thin slices
2 tablespoons toasted pinenuts
sprigs of fresh coriander

◆

1. To make the drop scone mixture, mix together the flour, cream of tartar and salt in a large bowl and beat in the eggs and a little of the soya milk to form a smooth cream. Beat in the rest of the soya milk and the ginger, spring onion and corn. Leave to stand.

2. To make the topping, blanch the vegetables by pouring boiling water over the carrots, cabbage and lemon grass. Leave to stand for three minutes. Drain well, and remove and discard the lemon grass. Use the liquid in soups or stock. Pour the soy sauce over the carrots and cabbage and keep warm.

3. Lightly brush a heavy frying pan with oil and heat well.

4. Stir the drop scone mixture and drop spoonfuls of the mixture onto the hot pan. Cook on one side for a minute or two until bubbles appear on the surface and the base is lightly browned.

5. Turn over and cook on the second side. Keep warm until all the mixture has been used up. Arrange on a warm plate and place two or three slices of smoked tofu on each pancake. Top with the blanched vegetables.

6. Serve sprinkled with the toasted pinenuts and garnish with coriander.

Grilled Vegetable and Goat's Cheese Pitta Parcels

LITTLE Gem lettuces and red peppers are available all the year round and both make excellent fillings for these substantial pitta parcels.

INGREDIENTS

4 Little Gem lettuces
4–5 tablespoons extra virgin olive oil
2 large red peppers, seeded and cut into large pieces
4 medium-sized round pitta breads

salt and freshly ground black pepper
225g (8oz) goat's cheese log, cut into slices
sprigs of fresh basil

1. Brush the lettuces with plenty of olive oil and cook under a hot grill until they are lightly seared. Turn over and brush with a little more oil. Cook until lightly browned. Remove from the heat and set aside.

2. Place the peppers, skin side up, under a hot grill and cook until well browned. Remove from the heat and leave to cool a little. Remove the skins if desired, though there is no necessity to do this.

3. Lightly toast the outside of the pitta breads under the grill. Split open and brush the inside with olive oil. Sprinkle with salt and pepper.

4. Fill the prepared pitta breads with the grilled vegetables and slices of goat's cheese. Add a few sprigs of basil and serve at once.

Celeriac Tortilla with Mushrooms

A TORTILLA makes a satisfyingly filling snack. You can eat it hot as soon as it is cooked, but if your appetite is not quite up to it you can leave it to cool and finish it off later. Add a tomato salad and a hunk of bread and the snack turns into a meal.

INGREDIENTS

½ medium-sized celeriac, peeled and finely diced

1 medium-sized potato, peeled and finely diced

1 onion, peeled and diced

3 tablespoons cooking oil

175g (6oz) brown mushrooms, wiped and sliced

8 eggs, beaten

2 tablespoons freshly chopped parsley

salt and freshly ground black pepper

1. Gently fry the celeriac, potatoes and onions in the oil over a medium heat for about 10 minutes, turning from time to time. Do not allow the vegetables to brown. Use a pan with a diameter of about 20–23 cms (7–8 inches).

2. Stir in the mushrooms and continue to fry for a further minute or two until the mushrooms soften.

3. Beat the eggs with the parsley and seasonings and pour over the vegetables. Stir and leave to cook over a low heat.

4. After 5–6 minutes the base should be cooked. Turn the tortilla over by placing a large plate over the pan and turning the tortilla onto it.

5. Slide the tortilla back into the pan to cook the other side. This will take another 5–6 minutes. Check that the vegetables are cooked through and cook for a little longer if need be.

6. Slide the cooked tortilla onto a hot serving plate and cut into four wedges.

Index

almonds:
  almond and herb rice, 92
  almond casserole dumplings, 77
  lemon bean and almond salad, 46
appetizers and canapés, 9–22
apples:
  beetroot with apples, 113
  cheese pâté with apples and walnuts, 42
  fennel, chicory and apple salad, 127
artichokes, soft lettuce salad with tapenade croûtons and, 43
asparagus and sweetcorn omelette, 106
aubergines:
  aubergine stuffed cabbage leaves, 117
  bhurta dip, 10
  stuffed marrow rings with aubergines and tomatoes, 103
avocados:
  avocado and pinenut crostini, 138
  avocado and sweetcorn canapés, 17
  taco salad, 129

bananas:
  curried banana toasts, 137
  curried green bananas with eggs, 81
  spiced banana biscuits, 19
basil:
  broccoli pesto sauce with taglialini, 107
  soupe au pistou, 48
beans see broad beans; red kidney beans etc
beansprouts:
  Thai soup with lemon grass and coriander, 25
beetroot:
  beetroot and orange salad with horseradish, 130
  beetroot with apples, 113
  quick winter borscht, 28
  taco shells with cauliflower and guacamole filling, 145
Belgian braised chicory with eggs, 101
bhurta dip, 10

biscuits, spiced banana, 19
borscht, quick winter, 28
bread:
  avocado and pinenut crostini, 138
  Brussel sprouts with nutmeg breadcrumbs, 115
  crostini porcini, 38
  soft lettuce salad with tapenade croûtons and artichokes, 43
  spicy cheese boats, 141
  see also sandwiches; toasts
brioche, chanterelles on toasted, 37
broad beans:
  broad bean and hazelnut soup, 30
  pasta shells with fresh beans and tomato sauce, 109
broccoli:
  broccoli chowder, 53
  broccoli hotpot, 76
  broccoli pesto sauce with taglialini, 107
  spicy broccoli with water chestnuts, 122
Brussel sprouts with nutmeg breadcrumbs, 115
Buddhist eggs, 142
bulgur wheat see cracked wheat

cabbage:
  aubergine stuffed cabbage leaves, 117
  egg and cabbage parcels, 99
  fennel and honey slaw, 126
  green cabbage salad, 124
  Hungarian cabbage pancake, 120
  sweet and sour cabbage soup, 54
caldo verde, Portuguese, 32
canapés and appetizers, 9–22
cannellini beans:
  Italian bean soup, 49
capers:
  egg and tarragon canapés, 18
  warm cauliflower and caper salad, 45
carrots:
  baked rutabaga and carrot pudding, 118

carrots (*continued*)
    carrot soup with curd cheese dumplings, 52
    egg and cabbage parcels, 99
    Hanseatic kohlrabi and carrots, 114
casseroles, 71–81
    almond casserole dumplings, 77
    broccoli hotpot, 76
    coconut bean stew, 73
    lentil and vegetable stew, 75
    mushroom goulash with noodles, 72
    Oriental vegetable casserole with okra, 74
    potato and celery stew, 78
    pumpkin and chickpea couscous, 80-1
cauliflower:
    crème Dubarry with leeks, 31
    Gujerati-style cauliflower, 84
    taco shells with cauliflower and guacamole filling, 145
    thick cauliflower and leek soup, 50
    warm cauliflower and caper salad, 45
celeriac:
    celeriac and ricotta filo pie, 63
    celeriac tortilla with mushrooms, 148
    celeriac with yogurt and potatoes, 121
    curried celeriac soup, 33
    Eastern fried rice with celeriac, 90
celery:
    potato and celery stew, 78
chanterelles on toasted brioche, 37
cheese, 5–6
    Buddhist eggs, 142
    cheese dreams, 20
    cheese pâté with apples and walnuts, 42
    crème Dubarry with leeks, 31
    fruity cheese parcels, 61
    Glamorgan sausages, 21
    Greek cheese and olives on toast, 139
    grilled vegetable and goat's cheese pitta parcels, 147
    Italian cheese and walnut salad, 134
    mushroom and cheese sauté, 140
    quesadillas, 144
    quick pan haggarty with sage, 98
    ravioli with sage and courgettes, 108
    soufflé mushrooms, 65
    Spanish stuffed tomatoes, 66
    spicy cheese boats, 141
    spinach bake with goat's cheese, 68

sweetcorn and Camembert soup, 59
tomatoes stuffed with Feta cheese, 16
cheese, soft:
    carrot soup with curd cheese dumplings, 52
    celeriac and ricotta filo pie, 63
    mushroom bites, 15
    olive and Mascarpone dip, 11
    polenta pie, 70
chestnuts:
    chestnut and orange soup, 35
    curried chestnuts, 83
    spinach and chestnut filo pie, 62
chickpeas:
    chickpea broth with coriander, 27
    Mexican mint and chickpea purée, 12
    noodles with chickpeas, tofu and coconut, 86
    pumpkin and chickpea couscous, 80-1
    Spanish Lenten soup, 29
    Spanish stuffed tomatoes, 66
    spicy stuffed peppers, 67
chicory:
    Belgian braised chicory with eggs, 101
    fennel, chicory and apple salad, 127
chillies:
    quesadillas, 144
Chinese fragrant soup, 24
chowder, broccoli, 53
coconut:
    coconut bean stew, 73
    noodles with chickpeas, tofu and coconut, 86
coriander:
    chickpea broth with coriander, 27
    Thai soup with lemon grass and coriander, 25
courgettes, ravioli with sage and, 108
couscous, pumpkin and chickpea, 80-1
cracked wheat:
    cracked wheat with okra, 93
    tabbouleh, 132
crème Dubarry with leeks, 31
crostini:
    avocado and pinenut, 138
    crostini porcini, 38
croûtons, tapenade, 43
curries:
    curried banana toasts, 137

curried celeriac soup, 33
curried chestnuts, 83
curried green bananas with eggs, 81
curried lentils, 112
Gujerati-style cauliflower, 84
mixed root vegetable curry, 79
Oriental vegetable casserole with okra, 74
sag aloo with greens, 82

dates:
curried banana toasts, 137
devilled mushrooms, polenta slices with, 104
dips:
bhurta, 10
olive and Mascarpone, 11
drop scones with smoked tofu and shredded
vegetables, 146
dumplings:
almond casserole dumplings, 77
curd cheese dumplings, 52

Eastern fried rice with celeriac, 90
eggs:
asparagus and sweetcorn omelette, 106
Belgian braised chicory with eggs, 101
Buddhist eggs, 142
celeriac tortilla with mushrooms, 148
curried green bananas with eggs, 81
egg and cabbage parcels, 99
egg and tarragon canapés, 18
egg and vegetable nests, 69
hard-boiled eggs in onion sauce, 100
Italian poached egg soup, 51
Oriental egg and tomato soup, 26
potato tortilla with creamed spinach, 105

fennel:
fennel and honey slaw, 126
fennel and olive tapenade, 14
fennel, chicory and apple salad, 127
fennel soup with goat's cheese, 58
flavourings, 5
French beans:
pasta shells with fresh beans and tomato
sauce, 109
fritters, Oriental sweetcorn, 39
fruit, 4
fruit and nut salad, 131
fruity cheese parcels, 61

garlic and tomato salsa toasts, 136
gingered neeps, 116
Glamorgan sausages, 21
goat's cheese see cheese
goulash, mushroom with noodles, 72
Greek cheese and olives on toast, 139
green beans:
lemon bean and almond salad, 46
green cabbage salad, 124
greens, sag aloo with, 82
guacamole:
taco shells with cauliflower and guacamole
filling, 145
Gujerati-style cauliflower, 84

Hanseatic kohlrabi and carrots, 114
hazelnuts:
broad bean and hazelnut soup, 30
horseradish:
beetroot and orange salad with
horseradish, 130
leek and horseradish salad, 128
hummus, grilled pepper ramekins with, 41
Hungarian cabbage pancake, 120

Indian mashed potato, 95
ingredients, 3-6
Italian bean soup, 49
Italian braised pumpkin, 119
Italian cheese and walnut salad, 134
Italian poached egg soup, 51
Italian risotto soup, 55

Japanese tofu canapés, 22

kale:
Portuguese caldo verde, 32
kidney beans:
bean purée on mini oatcakes, 13
coconut bean stew, 73
lemon bean and almond salad, 46
kohlrabi:
Hanseatic kohlrabi and carrots, 114
kohlrabi and red pepper salad, 133

leeks:
crème Dubarry with leeks, 31
Glamorgan sausages, 21
leek and horseradish salad, 128

leeks (*continued*)
  leek and mustard soup with mushrooms, 34
  thick cauliflower and leek soup, 50
lemon bean and almond salad, 46
lemon grass, Thai soup with coriander and, 25
Lenten soup, Spanish, 29
lentils:
  curried lentils, 112
  lentil and vegetable stew, 75
lettuce:
  soft lettuce salad with tapenade croûtons and artichokes, 43

mangetouts, watercress salad with, 44
marrow:
  stuffed marrow rings with aubergines and tomatoes, 103
Mexican mint and chickpea purée, 12
Mexican potato soup, 57
mint:
  Mexican mint and chickpea purée, 12
mushrooms:
  chanterelles on toasted brioche, 37
  chickpea broth with coriander, 27
  crostini porcini, 38
  leek and mustard soup with mushrooms, 34
  mushroom and cheese sauté, 140
  mushroom bites, 15
  mushroom goulash with noodles, 72
  polenta slices with devilled mushrooms, 104
  sesame stuffed mushrooms, 143
  soufflé mushrooms, 65
mustard:
  leek and mustard soup with mushrooms, 34

noodles:
  mushroom goulash with noodles, 72
  noodles with chickpeas, tofu and coconut, 86
  tomato noodle soup, 56
  vegetable noodles with nut sauce, 87
  warm spicy noodle salad, 88
nuts, 4
  fruit and nut salad, 131
  vegetable noodles with nut sauce, 87

oatcakes, bean purée on, 13
okra:
  cracked wheat with okra, 93
  Oriental vegetable casserole with okra, 74
olives:
  fennel and olive tapenade, 14
  Greek cheese and olives on toast, 139
  olive and Mascarpone dip, 11
omelette, asparagus and sweetcorn, 106
onions:
  hard-boiled eggs in onion sauce, 100
  quick pan haggarty with sage, 98
orange:
  beetroot and orange salad with horseradish, 130
  chestnut and orange soup, 35
  orange stir-fry vegetables with tofu, 102
Oriental egg and tomato soup, 26
Oriental sweetcorn fritters, 39
Oriental vegetable casserole with okra, 74

pan haggarty with sage, 98
parsley:
  tabbouleh, 132
pasta:
  broccoli pesto sauce with taglialini, 107
  pasta shells with fresh beans and tomato sauce, 109
  ravioli with sage and courgettes, 108
pâté, cheese with apples and walnuts, 42
peas:
  bhurta dip, 10
  shaken pease, 111
peppers:
  Buddhist eggs, 142
  grilled pepper ramekins with hummus, 41
  kohlrabi and red pepper salad, 133
  spicy stuffed peppers, 67
pesto:
  broccoli pesto sauce with taglialini, 107
pies:
  celeriac and ricotta filo pie, 63
  fruity cheese parcels, 61
  spinach and chestnut filo pie, 62
  tofu and tomato platter pies, 64
  see also pastries
pinenuts:
  avocado and pinenut crostini, 138
  broccoli pesto sauce with taglialini, 107

pistou, soupe au, 48
polenta:
    polenta pie, 70
    polenta slices with devilled mushrooms, 104
Portuguese caldo verde, 32
potatoes:
    broccoli chowder, 53
    celeriac with yogurt and potatoes, 121
    grated potato cakes, 94
    Indian mashed potato, 95
    Mexican potato soup, 57
    Portuguese caldo verde, 32
    potato and celery stew, 78
    potato, sweetcorn and spinach cake, 96
    potato tortilla with creamed spinach, 105
    quick pan haggarty with sage, 98
pumpkin:
    Italian braised pumpkin, 119
    pumpkin and chickpea couscous, 80-1
purées:
    bean purée on mini oatcakes, 13
    Mexican mint and chickpea purée, 12

quesadillas, 144

ravioli with sage and courgettes, 108
rice:
    almond and herb rice, 92
    Eastern fried rice with celeriac, 90
    Italian risotto soup, 55
    rice with sweetcorn, 91
    six jewel rice, 89
root vegetables:
    mixed root vegetable curry, 79
    quick winter borscht, 28
rutabaga and carrot pudding, 118

sag aloo with greens, 82
sage:
    quick pan haggarty with sage, 98
    ravioli with sage and courgettes, 108
salads, 123-34
    beetroot and orange salad with
        horseradish, 130
    fennel and honey slaw, 126
    fennel, chicory and apple salad, 127
    fruit and nut salad, 131
    green cabbage salad, 124
    Italian cheese and walnut salad, 134

kohlrabi and red pepper salad, 133
leek and horseradish salad, 128
lemon bean and almond salad, 46
mixed winter vegetable salad, 125
soft lettuce salad with tapenade croûtons
    and artichokes, 43
tabbouleh, 132
taco salad, 129
warm cauliflower and caper salad, 45
warm spicy noodle salad, 88
watercress salad with mangetouts, 44
sandwiches:
    cheese dreams, 20
sauce, broccoli pesto, 107
sausages, Glamorgan, 21
sesame seeds:
    sesame stuffed mushrooms, 143
    tofu sesame slices, 40
shaken pease, 111
six jewel rice, 89
snacks, 135-45
soufflé mushrooms, 65
soups, 23-35, 47-59
    broad bean and hazelnut soup, 30
    broccoli chowder, 53
    carrot soup with curd cheese dumplings,
        52
    chestnut and orange soup, 35
    chickpea broth with coriander, 27
    Chinese fragrant soup, 24
    crème Dubarry with leeks, 31
    curried celeriac soup, 33
    fennel soup with goat's cheese, 58
    Italian bean soup, 49
    Italian poached egg soup, 51
    Italian risotto soup, 55
    leek and mustard soup with mushrooms,
        34
    Mexican potato soup, 57
    Oriental egg and tomato soup, 26
    Portuguese caldo verde, 32
    quick winter borscht, 28
    soupe au pistou, 48
    Spanish Lenten soup, 29
    stock, 6-7
    sweet and sour cabbage soup, 54
    sweetcorn and Camembert soup, 59
    Thai soup with lemon grass and
        coriander, 25

soups (*continued*)
    thick cauliflower and leek soup, 50
    tomato noodle soup, 56
Spanish Lenten soup, 29
Spanish stuffed tomatoes, 66
spinach:
    potato, sweetcorn and spinach cake, 96
    potato tortilla with creamed spinach, 105
    sag aloo with greens, 82
    Spanish Lenten soup, 29
    spinach and chestnut filo pie, 62
    spinach bake with goat's cheese, 68
starters, 36–46
stews *see* casseroles
stock, 2–3, 6–7
supper dishes, 97–109
swedes:
    baked rutabaga and carrot pudding, 118
    gingered neeps, 116
sweet and sour cabbage soup, 54
sweetcorn:
    asparagus and sweetcorn omelette, 106
    avocado and sweetcorn canapés, 17
    Oriental sweetcorn fritters, 39
    potato, sweetcorn and spinach cake, 96
    rice with sweetcorn, 91
    sweetcorn and Camembert soup, 59

tabbouleh, 132
taco salad, 129
    with cauliflower and guacamole filling,
      145
taglialini, broccoli pesto sauce with, 107
tahini:
    sesame stuffed mushrooms, 143
tapenade:
    fennel and olive tapenade, 14
    soft lettuce salad with tapenade croûtons
      and artichokes, 43
tarragon:
    egg and tarragon canapés, 18
Thai soup with lemon grass and coriander,
    25
toasts:
    curried banana, 137
    garlic and tomato salsa, 136
    Greek cheese and olives, 139

tofu:
    aubergine stuffed cabbage leaves, 117
    drop scones with smoked tofu and
      shredded vegetables, 146
    Japanese tofu canapés, 22
    noodles with chickpeas, tofu and coconut,
      86
    orange stir-fry vegetables with tofu, 102
    tofu and tomato platter pies, 64
    tofu sesame slices, 40
tomatoes:
    garlic and tomato salsa toasts, 136
    Oriental egg and tomato soup, 26
    pasta shells with fresh beans and tomato
      sauce, 109
    polenta pie, 70
    quesadillas, 144
    Spanish stuffed tomatoes, 66
    stuffed marrow rings with aubergines and
      tomatoes, 103
    tofu and tomato platter pies, 64
    tomato noodle soup, 56
    tomatoes stuffed with Feta cheese, 16
tortilla, celeriac with mushrooms, 148
tortilla, potato with creamed spinach, 105
tortillas, quesadillas, 144

vegetables, 3–4, 110–22
    egg and vegetable nests, 69
    lentil and vegetable stew, 75
    mixed root vegetable curry, 79
    orange stir-fry vegetables with tofu, 102
    Oriental vegetable casserole with okra, 74
    six jewel rice, 89
    soupe au pistou, 48
    vegetable noodles with nut sauce, 87
    see also potatoes; tomatoes etc

walnuts:
    cheese pâté with apples and walnuts, 42
    Italian cheese and walnut salad, 134
water chestnuts:
    spicy broccoli with water chestnuts, 122
    warm spicy noodle salad, 88
watercress salad with mangetouts, 44

yogurt:
    bhurta dip, 10
    celeriac with yogurt and potatoes, 121